You've Only Got Three Seconds

Alana —
You will always fly
with the eagles. Enjoy
the trip!
Always charm your
audience — as a winner.

Fondly,
Camille

You've Only Got

Broadway Books

New York

CAMILLE LAVINGTON
With Stephanie Losee

Three Seconds

How to Make
the Right Impression
in Your Business
and Social Life

BROADWAY

A hardcover edition of this book was originally published in 1997 by Doubleday. It is here reprinted by arrangement with Doubleday.

Visit our website at www.broadwaybooks.com

First Broadway Books trade paperback edition published 2001.

Grateful acknowledgment is made for permission to reprint a scoring grid from *Please Understand Me: Character & Temperament Types* by David Keirsey & Marilyn Bates (Prometheus Nemesis, 1978).

The Library of Congress has cataloged the Doubleday hardcover edition of this book as follows:

Lavington, Camille.
    You've only got three seconds: how to make the right impression in your business and social life / Camille Lavington with Stephanie Losee.
      p.   cm.
    Includes index.
    1. Career development. 2. Social interaction. 3. Self-presentation. 4. Success in business. I. Losee, Stephanie. II. Title.
HF5381.L343 1997
650.1—dc20   96-24887
CIP

ISBN 0-385-48455-0

In memory of David Lavington

Acknowledgments

My sons, Chuck and David, fly with the eagles, for which I am deeply proud. This book is in tribute to their unconditional love, deep compassion, and wicked senses of humor.

Several talented people have inspired me to write this book, and I single out Jane Ciabattari for her generous contribution to my professional success. She has graciously shared her wisdom and expertise, since the first day we met, and so I pay special tribute to her.

Among those who stand beside me and never fail to add their encouragement, I want to especially thank: Liz Smith, Cheryl Mills, Barbara and Kirk Browning, Ann Hundley Chappel, Louise and Larry Crandall, Deborah Cole, Meredith Musick, Masa Isogai, Michael Lorelli, Patricia Peterson, James Serota, Mary Ellen Collins, Bonnie Blake, Lois Heenahan, Jean Jacullo, Jonathan Jensen, Kimberly Kleine, Dorothy Burke, Esther Carpenter, Betty Castro, Stanley Kober, Elaine Croteau, Harold Kooden, Walter Loeb, Maggie Lovaas, Joanne Mattera, Debora Midaneck, Rhoda Mintzer, Jeanne Moos, Tony Pratofiorito, Linda Richter, Anthony Russell, Stephanie Schus, Jim Shattuck, St. Clair Pugh, Charles Stieglitz, Jacquie Thompson, Natalie Tullman, Brian Archimbaud, Carolyn Gibbons Abernathy, Dick Ruffino, Jasmine Alexander, Jeffrey Wallin, Stanley Washington, Patricia White, Career Links members, and numerous others who have enhanced my life.

My special thanks to Traci Godfrey, for introducing me to my literary agent, Loretta Barrett, who shepherded my manuscript to Doubleday's talented editor Judith Kern. Judy's sensitivity has made the process a pleasure. I also acknowledge Stephanie Losee for helping me bring to fruition the book I have slaved over for several years.

Contents

Introduction

Enter a room, and it's already happened. Three seconds and you've been evaluated by everyone who saw you, even if all they did was give you a glance. They appraised your clothing and hairstyle. They noticed the way you carry yourself. They assessed your grooming and accessories. They observed as you greeted someone near the door. Three seconds have passed, and you've already made an indelible impression. Some people who watched you enter the room are intrigued; they've made a mental note to get to know you better. Others may have written you off.

It's a process that happens each time we meet someone new. In the first moments of the encounter we size each other up. We look for evidence that we have something in common. It happens in a flash, based entirely on surface cues, but we use this impression to make irreversible judgments. It works like this:

- If the person appears to be of comparable business or social level, he or she is considered suitable for further interaction.
- If he appears to be of higher business or social status, he is admired and cultivated as a valuable contact.
- If he appears to be of lower business or social standing, he is tolerated but kept at arm's length.
- If he is being interviewed, he either appears to match the corporate chemistry or he doesn't and it will affect the outcome.

These appraisals are being made constantly, in both business and social life. You've hardly said a word, but once this three-second evaluation is over, the content of your presentation can't change it. If you've made the best possible impression, you hold your audience in the palm of your hand. If you've made a poor impression, you've lost their attention—no matter how hard you work to get it back.

The choice is yours. You can be a victim of this process or you can learn to control the impression you make and modify it to suit any situation and come out a winner. Doing so requires a soul-searching analysis of your strengths and weaknesses, the desire to set a goal, and the discipline to change.

That's where I come in. I am founder and president of Camille Lavington and Associates, an international communications consulting firm based in New York City. Corporations and business executives hire me to teach them how to enhance their image. My clients range from top executives to mid-level personnel who learn how to take inventory of their personal strengths and vulnerabilities; balance their personalities; adjust their values; define career and social goals; determine what they'll need to do, say, and wear in order to fit the part; and take their internal and external makeover out into the world, ready to conquer every challenge.

In the past fifteen years I have been fortunate enough to counsel several thousand bright individuals. Some are stalled in frustrating jobs. Others seek my services to guide them through a difficult salary negotiation, to mount a job search, or to help them keep the job they already have. Companies retain me to groom executives for top management positions, tutor sales teams on the protocol required for international marketing, rectify a manager's personality problem, or polish a "comer" who's still a little rough around the edges. I resolve interdepartmental conflicts, write speeches, and show speakers how to command an audience's attention.

It's called "executive enhancement" and you don't have to clean out your bank account and hire a consultant to benefit from it. Using the techniques in this book, you can learn how to psych out others and tailor your approach to suit them in order to get what you want.

Initially clients are interested in applying my techniques to making favorable impressions in the business world, but they soon realize that much of what it takes to be successful in business is valuable in social settings as well. Indeed, impeccable manners, memberships in exclusive clubs or appointments to philanthropic committees, and the ability to move with ease among social tiers are vital characteristics of powerful people—in business *and* social life.

The challenge most people face is coming to terms with their shortcomings and finding out what is lacking in their interpersonal skills. This book is a wake-up call for those who haven't got a clue about their blind spots. My comments may make you wince and you may wish they weren't true, but let me assure you that, unless you accept these harsh truths about the rituals and mores of the business and social world, you will never be accepted. Those who do will have the advantage.

Personal marketing isn't about social climbing, nor is it about being artificial. Success comes to people who are versatile, who can make a smashing impression in any setting, who can identify their peers' or managers' hidden agendas, and use psychodynamics—the science of human behavior—to get what they want. Clients seek my counsel because I know what really goes on in and out of the office, and I tell it like it is without sugar-coating it. Like it or not, some bosses search their employees' offices after hours, or place enticing job ads in trade papers to see if any of their staffers are about to leave the company. Like it or not, many people make snap judgments about others to make themselves feel superior, and to save the time of dealing with those they don't consider their equals. If you want something from someone, you've got to get your foot past the door of those tyrannical three seconds.

It's time to level the playing field. Many people don't even realize that top executives have the advantage of being advised by a personal marketing consultant. Why shouldn't you have the same advantage?

Most people I counsel simply don't know how to think this way, and don't realize that others do. People who are savvy enough to follow these guidelines rise to the top of the business and social world. The ones who don't are what I call "well-intended innocents." Not knowing any better, they go along, doing their jobs, and seeing few results from their efforts because of the blind spot that keeps tripping them up. My job is to switch on the light that illuminates your blind spot, allowing you to see what others see.

According to the Scriptures, each of us is endowed with at least one God-given talent. Everyone must develop the confidence to cherish that gift and use it proudly. But talent is just half the equation; personality is the marketing half we all must develop to showcase our talent. You need to be able to do both—identify your strengths and master the personal style that will force people to pay attention to those strengths. As we approach the millennium and companies renounce their commitment to their workers, it requires ever greater political skills just to stay employed. I want you to move up, and nowadays that means wielding power like a CEO and kissing babies like a politician.

In this book you will follow the steps I use to help my clients reconfigure themselves, and you will learn to master and use the Ten Secrets of Power—a winner's attitude; a sense of self; an understanding of others; a loyal group of friends and associates; a powerful presence; a charming personality; the assurance to be self-promoting; the ability to negotiate to everyone's advantage; the instincts necessary to survive; and the ability to inspire and lead.

The first section will help you pinpoint your own temperament and perspective and teach you how to spot the secret agendas of others via a series of personality and bias tests. The tests will define your natural abilities, values, attitudes, motivations, socioeconomic comfort zones, prejudices—everything that has formed your point of view. Then you will progress to the quick-fix tactics, focusing on appearance and manners, that will signal the change in your perspective. Finally, I'll clue you in on the games going on in business, and teach you how to play so you too can move up the corporate or social ladder. The invisible barriers holding you back will vanish as you master the psychodynamics that influence upward mobility.

Our idealized world is a meritocracy in which hard work is the key to rising to the top of an organization, just like the proverbial cream. In the real world, however, it's the combination of connections, charm, and finesse that makes the cream rise. If you want those qualities, with discipline and application, they're yours.

You've Only Got Three Seconds

1

Welcome to the Real World

THEY'VE GOT YOUR NUMBER

Get used to it. The real world has your number. It only takes people three seconds to know where you're coming from. Within a few seconds they can size you up. It's not a comforting prospect to be judged so hastily, but that's the way it is.

Few people would claim that business and social interactions are pure and untainted, based exclusively on the content of each person's character. An interview, a business meeting, a social event—each is a kind of theater. You are an actor, playing your part as convincingly as possible in an effort to get the job, win over the client, or earn membership in the club. In actors' parlance, there are two ways to do it: method or technique.

Method acting requires the actor to *become* the character he's playing. If he has a scene in which he has to cry, he recalls a tragic incident from his own or the character's life to make himself feel sad. Technique acting, by contrast, is a way for the actor to portray feelings without actually having them. He learns the facial expressions that go along with anger, for example, and assumes those expressions so that he appears to be angry.

You'll combine method and technique acting to adjust your persona for different audiences. The inner being remains true to your values, but your demeanor, mannerisms, and wardrobe will shift as necessary. There's an old saying that a salesman is never selling a product, he's selling himself. If he's selling to a sophisticated European, he'll adopt Continental table manners and avoid asking personal questions. If he's selling to a Silicon Valley programmer, he'll dress casually and brush up on his Internet lingo. Throughout, he will be upbeat, warm, sincere, and gracious, successfully selling himself and his product by making others feel comfortable. If he addresses their need to receive a sales pitch from someone they can relate to, he's more likely to make the sale.

The good news is that you can influence people's perceptions of you by playing to their needs. Once you understand how to make other people feel comfortable with you, you've won their approval. There will always be differences, such as gender, that you cannot control, but aside from the obvious, you can work on ways to build rapport.

Here are the factors—other than skill—that influence people's reactions. In each case, we ask ourselves: "Does this person have similar attributes?" "Do we complement each other in some way?" "Is the chemistry right?" or "Are there too many obstacles to overcome?" Behind the doors and swept under the carpet are the differences and impressions that influence our emotional decisions.

DIFFERENCES AND IMPRESSIONS

Gender   Many people prefer to conduct business transactions with men.

Skin   The color of one's skin influences the bonding process.

Age   People are inclined to relate to those of a similar age.

Appearance   Status or class is defined by apparel, manner, and style.

Expression   People's facial expressions often reveal their attitude.

Eye contact   Direct eye-to-eye contact is expected in Western cultures; this is not the case in many Asian and African cultures.

Posture	Good bearing and carriage indicate positive self-worth.
Distance	People stand near or close depending on their cultures.
Touch	A firm handshake is normal in Western cultures. In some Eastern cultures, touching is not allowed.
Body odors	Personal hygiene is a high priority. Bad breath or body odors are offensive.

The first two characteristics are, of course, not subject to change. Moreover, there's no reason to dignify the reactions of bigots by engaging in a discussion of how to minimize the effect of gender or ethnicity in interactions where groups seek to exclude minorities. The other impression makers, however, are quite malleable, and it's worthwhile to use them to build bonds of commonality with anyone you want to influence or persuade. (I include age in this category because we should all do what we can to project an image of health and vitality in order to take age out of the equation in any encounter or negotiation.)

I stress that learning to manipulate the image you project isn't about being phony or pretending to be something you're not. It's about making your audience receptive to the *real you*. You're not forcing them to pay attention to your packaging. Rather, you're encouraging them to *go beyond* your packaging and pay attention to who you are and what you have to say. Your identity should not be confused with image power. The following descriptions will help you understand the difference.

IMAGE POWER

Identity is the substance people see and judge as they size you up to determine your status, power, and potential. It's the way others glean the essence of who you are by the way you present yourself; the things you say; the way you speak; and how you behave. Believe it or not, we project tangible clues that reveal our character or personality.

Image is the impression you make on others. It's the intangible quality you project that an audience responds to emotionally and intellectually. It's an opinion of you formed by someone who wants to believe, disbelieve, or ignore you based on his or her own class and value system.

Image Power is the sense of your potential and competence in the mind of the beholder, and the mind of the beholder is influenced by every detail of your appearance and manner. It's the implied potency you project that says you've been there, done that, and can handle the next challenge. It's the untested basis for another person's confidence in you before you perform.

You may not consider yourself a powerful person, but with the suggestions in this book you may come across as one. It's not as simple as buying a designer suit; my consulting business isn't a painting party where I spiff up my clients' exteriors. I start with their interiors, taking a holistic approach to helping them discover what causes them to behave in ways that hold them back.

Image is not skin deep. Anyone can walk into a room groomed to make a smashing impression, but there must be substance behind the delivery to sustain that impression. High ethical and moral standards must back up the impression you want to make.

It requires a change in mind-set—a process that can't be taken lightly.

EXECUTIVE ENHANCEMENT

Executive enhancement might sound narcissistic, but, in fact, it requires a great deal of character. It takes courage and unflinching self-evaluation. The object is to discover your blind spots—the aspects of your personality or behavior you're unaware of that restrict your ability to interact effectively with other people. It is when *others* uncover your blind spots that they are able to manipulate you. Once you understand *yourself* and make a commitment to self-discipline, you will:

- *Achieve a more balanced personality*
- *Accept your strengths or talents so you can begin to capitalize on them*

- *Identify your weaknesses in order to make a concerted effort to remedy them*
- *Protect your vulnerabilities from manipulation by others*
- *Learn to read people and situations so you can customize your communicating style accordingly*

Your goal is to make others feel comfortable around you by focusing on *them*. It takes a lot of time and research to figure out how to meet another person's needs. At first, it may seem that you're learning to put other people at ease simply in order to achieve your own goals. But what you'll discover is that being good to others is its own reward. Flying with the eagles means taking the high road in all things: your business life, your social life, your private life. As you rise professionally and socially, you'll have the latitude to influence others to follow your example and treat one another generously.

Case Study: Barry, Age 36

Barry was the number three executive at a national Wall Street insurance firm. He had come from a modest background and had struggled to pay for his Harvard Business School education. A gifted strategist and speech writer, Barry's behind-the-scenes contributions to the company were responsible for much of its financial success. Still, the chairman and CEO kept him sequestered in the back room when it came to introductions and high-level meetings with outside clients. These two Princeton grads from privileged backgrounds invited clients to play tennis and golf at a prestigious private club and took credit for the accounts Barry brought in—a simple maneuver since they never allowed him to close his own deals.

When Barry called to ask me for help, he had an insufferably arrogant attitude. He was so busy bragging about his Harvard smarts that it was clear he had no humility or social graces. Rather than acknowledge that we each had something to bring to the table, Barry let me know that he expected me to prove my value to him—an attitude I correctly assumed he adopted with everyone. He rambled on and on about inclusion and exclusion and about his interactions with people at higher levels, so I sensed that he had an inferiority complex and a chip on his shoulder so large it was a wonder he could stand up straight.

"Do you have a beard?" I asked over the phone. "Are you short? Is your wife at home caring for a baby when she isn't at a fancy department store spending 'your' money?" He replied yes in every case, surprised. I continued: "Do you feel that she bosses you around?" He answered: "Don't all women?"

I told Barry I wouldn't accept him as a client unless he was willing to change his attitude and clean up his act. He thought about it and called me back a few days later, saying he knew he needed to work with me and, if necessary, he'd even shave off his beard. (The first-impression perception of beards—right or wrong—is that they're a means of gaining attention for people who are trying to show that they're intellectually superior, professorial, nonconformist, or artistic. Oftentimes an aging bald man with a beard is seen as trying to establish his virility. Worse yet, business people in Asia consider men with facial hair to be lower-class. In any case, executives who wear beards do not bond with many people; it's a way to put them off.)

For our first meeting, Barry arrived at my office with a single cup of coffee in a brown paper bag. Clearly he was accustomed to taking care of his own needs without considering the needs of others. Think of it: wouldn't you expect the person whose office you're visiting to offer you coffee? And if you made the odd choice of bringing your own, wouldn't you buy an extra cup to offer your colleague?

I asked Barry what amenities he had expected me to share with him as my guest, and what level of consideration he thought I should expect of him. Barry rationalized his behavior: he'd never met me before, figured I could take care of myself, didn't want to put me to any bother, thought he didn't owe me anything yet. I explained that in certain social situations a childish insistence on doing everything yourself can be self-centered and inconsiderate. Being political starts with being polite.

Barry took my suite of psychological and bias tests (you'll find these later in this book), which revealed:

- Having pulled himself up by his bootstraps through education, Barry believed that as long as he did his work he'd get a good grade. He never worried what kind of paper his report was on, as it were, or how he packaged it.
- He discounted the value of social skills, preferring to assert his intellectual superiority rather than seek ways to make others comfortable. He didn't think social amenities were at all worthwhile. No wonder everybody kept him behind the barn!
- Barry always focused on what he was getting out of every situation, never what he was putting in.
- He was a big fault-finder, so I asked him to keep a running list of the things he liked about his job and his colleagues just to get him off the negative kick.

I began teaching Barry how to push his "up button" instead of his "down button" so he could ride the elevator to the top of his career instead of plummeting toward the basement. Barry complained of lack of recognition, so when he went out of town to a convention attended by many of the firm's customers, I suggested he throw a big dinner party the first or second night with his boss, the CEO. I knew full well that his boss would never allow him to be the host of a party for clients, so I told him in advance that, when his boss said no, he should counter by explaining that he understood the budget limitations and would instead take a few people out for drinks toward the end of the week. Since Barry had told me his boss would leave the convention by midweek, I asked him to give a cocktail party by written invitation the following night. When people arrived and asked for the absent CEO, Barry was to reply: "You know the boss stays only a couple of days and wouldn't want me to throw a big dinner, so I decided you all mean so much to me that I'd throw a little cocktail party to thank you for your business." I told Barry to do his best to land a new client during the convention and, if not, to elicit some kind of praise he could bring back to the office with him and use to his advantage.

I directed Barry to go to the chairman and CEO when he returned to the office and share his good news. In the course of bragging, he slipped in the information that he had given a cocktail party for the company's clients, acting as upbeat as possible so as not to invite a reprimand from the CEO. This was his way of saying: "Don't keep me in the back room, fellas, I won't stand for it." By encouraging him to take this initiative, I also helped him break his fear of going up against the CEO and chairman.

Barry went to his office over the weekend and got rid of boxes, stacks of newspapers, and old coat hangers. He put a pile of paperwork on his secretary's desk to alert her that something unusual was happening. I told him to look at all of his overdue reports and make a To Do list, giving a copy to his secretary, with the intention of catching up on those tasks pronto. (Secretaries gossip to more senior secretaries as a form of wielding power, so this was one of the best information hotlines Barry could tap into.) The point of all this activity was to unsettle the two senior officers. They'd observe his new self-confidence and the visual change in his office, and assume he was preparing to leave the company.

Next I had Barry order a large ficus tree to be delivered to his office—a sign of permanence and stability. The reason? Remember B. F. Skinner's famous perception studies with pigeons: Skinner found that if he fed all his pigeons at the same hour each day, they would approach their feeding tray at the correct time. When he changed the time once, the pigeons adjusted their schedule. But when he changed the time again, the pigeons never knew what to expect and were unable to adapt.

By the same token, Barry's activities were intended to make the chairman and CEO uneasy and unable to return to their original sense of him. In the meantime, we were making changes in his hairstyle and wardrobe to bring him up to the level of dress and appearance of the people who were his peers and superiors, further signaling that drastic changes were taking place.

Months in advance of bonus time, I coached Barry to engineer some sort of coup that contributed to his company's bottom line. Once he had accomplished it, he met with both his superiors at the same time so that they couldn't play off each other, and informed them of his contribution, alerting them to the fact that he expected to be compensated for such innovations. In the months leading up to bonus time, he brought up this idea from time to time to plant the seed in their heads, nurturing its growth until it blossomed.

In most companies it takes six months for a dramatic change to take effect—you can't reform someone's idea about a bonus or promotion overnight. Not only do such changes take time, they require repetition. Psychologists have found that an idea heard once is forgotten within twenty-four hours, and the concept doesn't penetrate until it's repeated eight times.

Well ahead of the delivery date, Barry began asking his superiors to plan on giving him a well-earned and much-increased bonus and a new title; money doesn't mean much unless the marketplace can see objectively that your company has granted you the recognition that goes with a new title. In addition, Barry asked his superiors to underwrite his initiation fees and dues at the Harvard Club in New York as well as to sponsor his membership at a prestigious private club.

The results? Barry was promoted to senior vice-president and received a significant bonus—nearly double the $225,000 he was expecting. He now belongs to the Harvard Club, and his membership at another of New York's exclusive clubs gives him the ear of some of the most influential people in the city. Barry had gone from a bitter back-office drone to a visible, respected, productive, top-ranking officer of the company.

Barry's story took place at the top of a prominent insurance firm, but the methods I taught him to maximize his assets and transform his image are the same ones that could be used to get promoted out of the mail room. This success story demonstrates an important point: there is a way to overturn that deadly three-second first impression. Barry's superiors thought they'd pegged him long ago, but he shook things up so much that he created a new Barry, one they'd have to meet for the first time. The chairman and CEO were forced to discard their previous impression of him and reevaluate.

Perhaps after reading about Barry you feel uncomfortable with the concept of making changes in your persona to control other people's perceptions of you. If that's the case, consider this: regardless of how you feel about the fairness of treating people better or worse on the basis of their image, others are doing it to you. Why not know the rules and learn how to package yourself in order to succeed in your chosen environment? Whether you acknowledge it or not, you are blatantly showcasing how you feel about yourself with every gesture. Why allow others to know more about how you come across than you do?

Moving ahead is like choosing your seat on an airplane. Within the plane are three tiers of service: first class, business class, and coach. In each section you're served differently and you act accordingly. In first class, flight attendants hand out linen napkins and serve meals on china plates. They offer all the amenities: a reclining seat, blankets and pillows, the latest newspaper, a Perrier refill every time you empty your glass. In coach, children fidget, you get a pack of peanuts, and you scramble for an old magazine with half the pages torn away.

This analogy doesn't mean you have to aspire to the first-class section, or that you have to believe that the money people pay to sit there is money well spent. But if you lack the ability to feel comfortable in any class, be it first class, business class, or coach class, if you don't know how to adapt your behavior to the different sections, you're stuck in one section only.

Your life experiences until now have either enhanced or limited your ability to move comfortably among the sections of the airplane—that is to say, among the power groups of a company, where titles delineate rank, or among different social levels, which are divided by behavior. Learn how to adjust your behavior to suit any situation and you're free to sit anywhere.

I teach clients how to fly with the eagles rather than swarm with the mosquitoes, but that doesn't mean scorning people who are a step lower on the business or social ladder. In fact, flying with the eagles means precisely the opposite—it means being generous, contributing more than you take, helping others to achieve their goals. It means being secure enough to move comfortably around many levels and adjust to any environment, any audience, rather than stepping on heads in your quest for upward mobility.

THE POWER OF A GENEROUS SPIRIT

A phrase that comes up often when I'm explaining my program to clients is "Be gracious and acknowledge others." It's the simplest expression of what it requires to fly with the eagles. If you call a busy person on the phone, don't jump right in and start talking. Be gracious: say a warm hello, identify yourself, and ask how the person is feeling. Acknowledge: tell him you know he's busy and ask if this is a good time to talk. Another example? If you make a mistake at work, don't get defensive. Be gracious: keep your frustration to yourself and don't take it out on the person who detected your error. Acknowledge: fess up to the mistake, explain what will prevent it from happening again, and move on.

The same phrase covers social circumstances. Say a friend has been diagnosed with a health problem and some of the people in his circle feel so uncomfortable about the situation that they're avoiding him. Be gracious: call and invite him to join you for dinner. Acknowledge: offer to do a chore to help him out during this difficult time. If you're getting married and can't include a close friend in the wedding party? Don't dodge your friend's questions or behave as if there is no issue between you. Be gracious and acknowledge: tell her that you value her friendship, but you must restrict your bridal party to family members only. Then invite her to the rehearsal dinner so that she will feel special.

The art of being gracious and acknowledging others is nothing more than the ancient Chinese philosophy of saving face. Help someone to save face in any given situation and you have preserved, rather than broken, a bond. It's not a quality easily cultivated by people who are only out for themselves. Like the five points of a star, acts of empathy, deference, reciprocity, acknowledgment, and acquiescence make you burn brighter. It's naive to overlook simple gestures that build loyal followers.

Like Fezziwig, Ebenezer Scrooge's benevolent old boss in *A Christmas Carol,* a successful business person gets that way by making others feel good about themselves and their workplace.

Fezziwig, you may remember, had a work-hard, play-hard attitude that energized his young apprentices. Each of us has had a Fezziwig in our lives—a teacher or boss for whom we had high regard and whom we wanted to please. Think of the result of this kind of leadership. Fezziwig wasn't a pushover, he was a hard-driving businessman who got results from his employees. At the same time, he had the satisfaction of knowing that the people who worked for him enjoyed what they did. He was encouraging their well-being and success, which only made his own business more profitable. Plus he was respected, even loved. Once he was boss, Scrooge's nasty demeanor didn't inspire any better results—it certainly didn't earn him anyone's esteem.

In the eighties especially, we moved away from a positive leadership paradigm. It was more popular for CEOs to be *un*popular, to be thought of as ruthless and bottom-line oriented. It was the era of bloody LBOs (leveraged buyouts) and nice guys finishing last. Indeed, nice guys without street smarts or political savvy have a way of watching others climb the ladder while they remain stuck on the bottom rung. But nice guys who keep an eye on their own agendas while enabling others to be successful build a constituency of supporters who keep their ascendancy going. Without such a constituency, not-nice guys tend to get eaten alive when they slip and fall off the ladder into shark-infested waters. Wall Street coffins are filled with such pompous casualties.

If you offer your talents selflessly and assist others to reach the pinnacle of their own power, everyone is enriched by the magnitude of talents. The perception of your power becomes a reality when it's given away and enables everyone to soar to new heights. In this book I'll teach you everything you need to know in order to do that.

THE TEN SECRETS OF POWER

If you follow these basic tenets in your approach to life, you will be more successful in social and business settings.

1. A Winner's Attitude, a Positive Outlook

- Have the confidence to expect acceptance from others, an appreciation of your talents, and high compensation. This requires caring about yourself and meeting your own standards of excellence.
- Build your credibility by enhancing your reputation with solid performances, rather than by currying favor.

2. Self-Awareness of Your Talents and Abilities

- What matters is not the absolute size of your contribution to life but how you use what you are given.
- You are the steward of your talents, not their owner. Accept that you are entrusted with one or more talents and that you have a duty to manage those gifts to produce a return for whoever gave them to you. Talents must be shared; they are not for you alone.

3. Understand Others

- Ascertain another person's personality type and psychosocial profile.
- Customize your selling style. The power of persuasion starts when you get in sync with another person's values.

4. Build a Power Base with Friends in Power

- Protect your flanks with loyal friends and associates who admire, respect, and support you when you aren't around to defend yourself.
- Senior executives often hold your destiny in their hands, so find mentors in high places who can influence decisions.

5. Stage a Performance and Package Your Presentation

- Look the part by dressing to the level of power you aspire to achieve.
- Your speech conveys your mood, authority, and sense of purpose.
- State your points clearly and concisely.

6. Charm the World and Praise Others

- Recognize talent and express gratitude for top performance and competence at all levels. Even the boss likes to hear praise!

7. Engage in Unabashed Self-Promotion

- Campaign for yourself—don't follow the example of John Alden.

- Write articles and give speeches at every opportunity to gain visibility.

8. Negotiate So Everyone Wins
- Give an advantage in order to win. Set the starting point high and prepare to come down to salve the other person's ego.
- Keep a poker face. Remain professional and detached to hold an advantage over the unknown.

9. Use Your Instincts and Street Smarts
- Employ psychodynamics to pinpoint people's hidden agendas and power games.
- Hone your political skills and keep your own counsel—the walls have ears.
- Timing makes a difference, so take one step at a time. Recognize when it's wise to hold an opinion or keep a judgment to yourself.

10. Inspire and Lead
- Dedicate your efforts as if you owned the business by being conscientious, diligent, and honorable.
- Share the glory, allowing others to take the credit occasionally so you are perceived as a fair and decent person.
- You must nurture and encourage the development of the people entrusted to you, whether they are your children or your subordinates. As Kahlil Gibran wrote in *The Prophet,* "You are the bows from which your children as living arrows are sent forth."

THREE-SECOND OVERVIEW

Whether we like it or not, critics are everywhere just waiting to pass judgment. If you want to win their favorable endorsement, in order to advance your career, it's wise to follow the Ten Secrets of Power.

In the next chapter you'll discover some thought-provoking ways to know yourself better. I'll show you how to pinpoint your values and help you to understand how those values motivate your behavior so you can begin to focus your campaign.

2

What Do You Value?

YOUR PERSONAL MISSION STATEMENT

Any corporation of merit in business today identifies a mission from which arise all its strategies and activities. A mission statement is a declaration of values, goals, and positioning.

Before you take one more step, you must identify your own mission and determine your own values. It's time to explore your perspective, or how you view the world.

Values determine our personal bias and influence behavior, so becoming aware of them is essential to identifying the blind spots that keep us from getting ahead or getting along. When I ask new clients to be prepared to adjust their values, I don't mean that they should compromise their ethics. Values aren't virtues or morals, they're the beliefs that shape a person's point of view, and those beliefs do change. Staying true to them can limit people to function in only one stratum of power.

To help my clients figure out their point of view and attitude, I give them a series of values tests. Once they understand their values, they can decide whether to reexamine them. Then they can go on to figure out where *others* are coming from and shift gears to adapt to any situation and impress or influence the people involved.

Understanding your value system can also help you figure out what would make you happier in the workplace and in social life. A telemarketer who works at home but discovers through values tests that he places a premium on interactions with others might consider switching to a job in a busy office. An administrator whose tests indicate she ranks money low on her list of priorities might ask herself whether she's sending out signals that tell her employer he can get away with paying her less than she's worth. Armed with that insight, she can use the tactics I'll describe in Chapter 6 to change her employer's perception of her and get the raise she deserves.

These are just two examples of how an awareness of values can enhance your professional and private life. Most important, this awareness can help you enhance the lives of others, and that's the very basis of my program. We can work to advance our careers and improve our social lives, but in the end the best way to achieve our goals is to help other people achieve theirs. Being successful is about being decent, adding more to the pot than you take out of it. If you make an effort to discern the values of someone on your team, you can try to find a way to give that person what pleases or motivates him—without compromising your ethics. It will benefit you as well by creating good will in your workplace and enhancing your reputation.

I ask all of my clients to read Machiavelli's *The Prince,* published in 1532, because it is a discourse on how to wield power. Fighting for control of a company—or even of a department— might not seem comparable to the struggles Machiavelli addresses, but the tactics are the same and can get just as ugly. Doing good deeds may seem like a way to get stepped on rather than promoted at the office, but Machiavelli teaches that being nice and pleasing people can help you control them. Being gracious and generous also happens to be the right thing to do, and it's something you want to continue to do when you've achieved success. When your cup is flowing over, you want to give others the excess.

Giving to others and getting what you want are not incompatible, in fact they are two sides of the same coin. An example is the Chinese theory that you never start a war, you never let your opponent lose face, and you never lose power. If you never start a war, you don't allow yourself to dwell in the trenches—to adopt negative ways of achieving your goals. If you never let your opponent lose face, you've saved his dignity while making him inclined to compromise with you. Throughout, you've retained your power by taking the high road.

A WINNER'S ATTITUDE: POWER SECRET #1

Values determine attitude, and attitude can limit our possibilities or broaden them. The classic role triangles pictured, used by many self-help groups, illustrate the two basic attitudes people adopt and show how those attitudes determine the way they approach life.

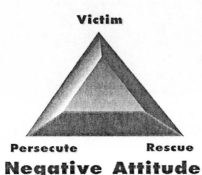

Victim

Persecute   **Rescue**

Negative Attitude

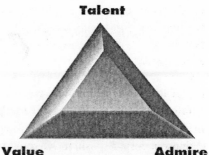

Talent

Value   **Admire**

Positive Attitude

Each of us has to ascertain which triangle we fit into and whether we want to change. The person with a positive viewpoint wants to be accepted for her talent, her warmth, her contribution to life. The negative individual makes herself either the victim, the persecutor, or the rescuer by engaging in neurotic relationships. People who fit into the latter category can learn to adopt a more positive attitude, and positive thinkers can learn to spot negative thinkers to avoid being drawn into a codependency role.

In particularly cutthroat business settings, people in power exploit persecutors by turning them into henchmen to do their dirty work. Sometimes powerful people reinforce the negativity of a persecutor by allowing him to criticize an employee's performance so that the employee feels he is not worthy of climbing the ladder.

The illustrations are aimed at ferreting out specific information about point of view, but the answer to almost any question will reveal volumes about a person's basic values and attitudes. Let's say, for example, you are meeting an acquaintance or business associate for lunch, and it's a gray day. Your lunch partner is late. When he arrives, you ask, "Is it raining out there?"

Response 1

"Yes, it's raining cats and dogs," he says. "But after all of these months of dry weather, we really need it. I hope you haven't been waiting long."

This is the reaction of a person with a positive attitude. He acknowledges that the rain is heavy but comes up with a reason why it's not such a bad thing, then turns the conversation around to you.

Response 2

"What a rainstorm, like cats and dogs. I thought I'd never be able to get a cab, so I took the bus and got caught in traffic. I'm sorry I'm a little late."

This is also a positive person, who is considerate enough to explain his lateness without going into too much detail, apologizes, then gets off the subject.

Response 3

"Like cats and dogs. You wouldn't believe how windy it is out there. I must have waited at least fifteen minutes for a cab, and when I flagged one down some jerk ran around me and stole it. Then I figured I would get the subway instead, but when I went through the turnstile my umbrella broke. So I tried to buy one from this guy selling them down there, and he charged me ten bucks! I wasn't about to pay him that much. Then the subway was backed up and we got stuck between stations for ten minutes waiting for this train ahead of us to move. I finally had to walk here from the station twelve blocks away. Now I'm soaked."

You won't be surprised to learn that this is the response of a negative person. Not only does he neglect to apologize for his tardiness, he makes you take care of his emotional needs by dumping his sob story on you and prompting you to console him about his misadventure and wet clothing. Before lunch even begins, you're depleted.

Listening to a person's positive or negative reaction to events of the day will give you insight into his or her attitude. Stay away from those who operate from the negative triangle as victims, rescuers, or persecutors!

During conversation, I listen to hear whether my associate introduces a topic we're both interested in or starts talking about himself. Does he prattle on about a subject that can't be shared? Politics, religion, sex, illness, accidents, and death all fall into this category, especially if the person is focused only on his own experience. Many people volunteer information about their personal strife to impress you with how much adversity they've overcome. Others ask a lot of questions to pump you and don't share information. Some people never learned the etiquette of group conversation, neglecting to introduce you, bring you into the loop, get you a chair, or do something else that would make you feel comfortable.

All of us will listen to anyone discuss any topic as long as he tries to make a connection, takes care of our emotional needs, acknowledges our skills, shows he's been in our position, or demonstrates he might know someone we'd like to meet. But if he just barrels ahead, it doesn't matter if he's Einstein returned from the dead—we won't listen. In the end, such people don't offer any evidence that they value *others,* and that's what everyone responds to.

One day I passed a small shirt store and asked the salesman to tell me the history of the clothing phenomenon of the moment—periwinkle-blue chambray shirts. I explained that I was a corporate image builder who often made recommendations to clients about their wardrobes. The salesman asked the owner of the store to call me, and we chatted briefly before I commented: "I've noticed all the Wall Streeters wearing these shirts. They seem to have started a trend."

"That's your opinion," she said curtly, changing the tone of the conversation. "It started a long time ago with dress-down day."

I was genuinely taken aback. I'll never know why she cut me down like that. Perhaps I had unwittingly hit a nerve. She might have been fired from a Wall Street job at one time—it could be anything. The point is that she broke the bridge we were building and did herself out of the boost I could have given her shop by sending my clients to her. The negative personality always looks for trouble instead of looking for opportunities.

That's what each encounter can be—an opportunity. You never know who someone is, or whom they know, or how they can help you. Bonding with people helps you persuade them when the time comes. Remember, Republicans don't talk to Democrats until they get into Congress. Politicians are a good example of the way positive, powerful people can benefit from helping others. Members of Congress do good deeds for one another partly so they can call in favors when they need extra votes. In assisting one another and getting their own bills passed, their constituents may be helped too. Everyone wins.

VALUES AND JUDGMENTS

Have you ever wondered what drives us to the decisions that affect our lives? Value judgments color our perspective and motivate us to behave in a particular way. They can constrict or enhance our ability to maximize opportunities.

To discover value judgments there are many tests designed by psychologists. Let's start with an old favorite: The Couple in the Tropics. This classic test is fun because it cuts right to the heart of people's values, but its content is so dicey, it sometimes gets their backs up. Try not to focus on the nature of the story but on the points of view the story illustrates. And a note for the men: the protagonist is a woman in a plight that doesn't generally befall men, but try to see her impartially as one of the players instead of placing undue emphasis on her gender.

There was a couple who lived happily on two tropical islands connected by a bridge. One day a violent hurricane washed away the bridge and destroyed nearly all the foliage. When the storm

passed, the man and woman discovered they were on separate islands with no way of crossing the shark-infested waters between
them. The man took inventory of his situation and found that there
was one other survivor on his island, and no remaining trees. The
woman looked around and observed that there were two other survivors and a lone palm tree on her island. The man and woman
yelled across the water to each other and quickly came to the conclusion that the only way they could be reunited was for the woman
to use the tree as a bridge.

The woman turned to one of the survivors on her island and
asked for his help in uprooting the tree. "That's a lot of work," the
man said. "What can you offer me in payment?" The woman
replied that she had nothing to give him. "I believe in an even
exchange," he said, thinking like a typical businessman. The
woman turned to the other survivor and asked him for his help
instead. "I'm a botanist," he said. "I'd like to be left alone to
study the plants."

Despairing, the woman returned to the businessman. "What
would it take to get you to help me?" she asked. The businessman
thought for a moment. "You're the only woman on this island," he
said. "I think an evening of your favors would be fair compensation." She rejected his offer and complained to the botanist.
"Make up your own mind," he answered. "It doesn't matter to me
what you do. Be responsible for your own actions."

After giving a lot of thought to her limited options, the woman
accepted the businessman's proposition. The next morning he cut
down the palm tree and used it to serve as a bridge across the
lagoon as he had promised. Reunited with her beau at last, the
woman explained the sacrifice she had made to rejoin him. "You
did *what?*" the indignant suitor said, and scorned her.

The older man approached the heartsick woman. "Don't be so
hard on yourself," he told her. "You wanted to be with him, and
you made the only choice possible to join him."

To take the test, rank the characters from 1 to 5 in terms of their
value or merit. Which player's actions are the most acceptable to
you, and which the least? There are no right or wrong answers.

Here's how to translate your responses.

A = Egoist   You are in charge of your own destiny
B = Mercenary   You exchange services for payment
C = Isolationist   You are a self-centered individualist
D = Moralist   You judge others and yourself
E = Humanitarian   You are tolerant and less judgmental

People who rank the young woman (A) high on their list have good self-worth. They feel they can control their lives and their destiny. The person who is tolerant of the woman's actions understands that people have to make compromises, but they get out of life what they put into it.

Those who rank the businessman (B) highly look at life as a series of exchanges. No favor is done without expectation of reciprocity, and services are valuable commodities to be traded.

The test taker who looks favorably upon the isolationist (C) likes to mind his own business and resents intrusions. This answer can indicate a career predilection in the fields of science, computers, math, or research—something that requires total concentration and solitude.

People who choose the older man (E) are kindhearted realists who accept others as they are. These are the tolerant liberals who should consider pursuing politics or charitable work. Many women put this character in the top half of their lists.

Finally, there's the young suitor (D). Those who rank him highly can sometimes be inflexible; they're not usually tolerant of those who follow a different code of ethics, and they tend to see things in black and white. Often they were raised in a structured, religious environment. Alternatively, people with a tolerance for the moralist might be very young and idealistic.

You can see that this test is a fine diagnostic tool with a small drawback: people who would have been sympathetic to the businessman's interests if he had asked the woman for something less offensive than spending the night with him might rank him lower than he deserves. Still, my clients find that they quickly learn so much about their values by taking this test that I prefer to give it first.

FUNDAMENTAL HUMAN NEEDS

A way to think about what motivates people is to imagine a personal scale that is balanced by the need for "recognition" at one end and the desire for "pleasure" on the other end, with "survival" as the base. At times one end may tip up and the other end may decline, but the need for survival is always the most overpowering need. You will be more personally fulfilled if you maintain a balance.

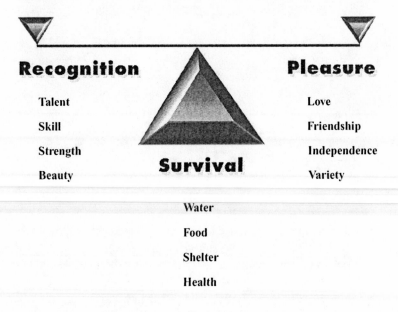

Recognition

Talent

Skill

Strength

Beauty

Survival

Pleasure

Love

Friendship

Independence

Variety

Water

Food

Shelter

Health

WHAT MOTIVATES YOU?

Marketing specialists target their campaigns to answer a need within the three categories of survival, pleasure, and recognition. Their object is to trigger your "hot button" so you will respond to one of their sales campaigns. When I was the advertising director of a major consumer products company, I scanned a list of motivational incentives for promotional ideas. Now I use them to help people discover more about themselves and their human needs. You may learn more about what motivates you by scanning the following list.

Economic Goals

To preserve wealth and rank
To attain wealth and status
To build a rewarding career
To achieve financial security
To win the advantage in negotiations or transactions
To make money
To save money

Interpersonal Relationships

To gain power to lead: in government, business, organizations
To triumph over a competitor or adversary
To gain career advancement
To gain personal recognition
To gain sexual appeal
To love and be loved
To impress people
To have friends
To fulfill obligations
To help relatives, friends, and the less fortunate

Frame of Mind

To enjoy intellectual, emotional, and personal freedom
To achieve sexual gratification
To alleviate negative thoughts—such as stress, fear, shame
To fill voids caused by boredom or loneliness
To avoid risks and to allay fears
To build self-confidence and self-esteem
To be spiritually delivered

Life of Ease

To avoid labor
To make life more comfortable
To eliminate inconveniences
To relieve time pressures with timesavers

Personal Enrichment

To become more knowledgeable or better educated

To enhance mental powers and sense of logic
To improve memory
To become more persuasive
To become more charming
To enrich cultural knowledge
To enhance creative talents
To enhance personal appearance
To improve health
To become stronger
To behave in a socially acceptable manner
To dress fashionably
To manage time
To learn useful skills

Entertainment and Pleasure

To enjoy life's pleasures and fun
To be sexually active
To be adventurous
To gamble or take risks
To be mentally stimulated
To enjoy visual pleasures
To listen to music
To touch surfaces
To smell fragrances
To savor flavors

When people start talking to me—whatever the circumstance—I sort their responses into whether they're motivated by the need for recognition, survival, or pleasure. Everyone is motivated by different things; when you're aware of other people's preferences you can better understand how to relate to them and customize your approach to them. We all want to be enriched by our daily exchanges with others—the person who loses out is the one who doesn't recognize and listen to the other person's point of view. When you're with someone who doesn't stimulate you, the interaction goes nowhere.

People who are motivated by the need for recognition don't like being anonymous. This is someone who goes beyond her current job duties—she runs for office, volunteers to head a committee, or tries to move up the ladder of an organization. She might be a name-dropper or a self-promoter who talks about her aspirations and achievements.

Someone who's motivated simply to survive is content to work at the post office until he can get a pension, or perhaps at some repetitive factory job that doesn't teach him anything new but pays the bills. This is the least sophisticated level of work—a job with no brain food. Everyone needs sustenance, but there are different ways to nourish yourself. Some people want caviar and fine wines, while others are happy with macaroni and cheese. A survivor's conversation is peppered with references to working nine to five, following systems, or refusing to take work home. This is a reactive rather than proactive personality.

Pleasure seekers talk more about their vacations or after-hours activities than about their work. Stories are filled with detailed sensory descriptions—the cashmere sweater he had to have because it felt so good, the spicy fish eaten at a restaurant with glamorous atmosphere. Oftentimes pleasure seekers are more affluent and can afford to sate their senses; if they aren't, they sometimes allow their careers to go off track while they stimulate their senses at pleasure zones like bars or casinos.

What motivates you?

THE QUICK LIST TEST

This is a variation on a test used by Dr. Joyce Brothers. The point of the test is to answer without overthinking your responses and to skip any question that gives you trouble. Where a question requests the name of a person, choose anyone you'd like, past or present, real or fictional.

1. Name a leader you respect.
2. Name someone whose career or lifestyle you admire.
3. Name a friend or family member you are close to.
4. Name someone you'd like to exchange lives with.
5. Where in the world would you like to live?

6. Recount a negative experience and a positive experience from childhood.

7. Describe three favorable comments made about you.

As I give this test to my clients, I ask them to go down the list and explain their responses to me. What qualities does this leader possess? What about this person's career do they admire? What makes this childhood memory so special? As you ask yourself why you gave these answers, write the rationales next to your responses. What do they reveal about your dreams, hopes, desires?

It's impossible to interpret every possible response, so as illustration I'll analyze the test completed by a female business executive and philanthropist in her sixties.

1. *Napoleon.* The consultant explained that she chose him because he was a clever strategist able to motivate people beyond the norm.

2. *Goodwill ambassador and socialite Brooke Astor.* "She interfaces with people who are concerned about world issues and privately entertains on a grand scale."

3. *Her cousin Michael.* "He is compassionate, simpatico, and objective. We have a similar point of view and value system, and I am pleased with the longevity of our relationship and the acceptance I get from him."

4. She couldn't answer this question because she couldn't think of anyone she'd rather be. "I like the life I've got, as painful as it can sometimes be."

5. *Paris.* "It's beautiful, sophisticated, and offers tremendous variety of experience." (She currently lives in New York City.)

6. The consultant remembered being singled out for a special program at school. Her negative experience was her mother's disloyalty when the activity went awry.

7. "I've been told that I am compassionate, sophisticated, and shrewd."

This client follows the usual pattern of listing people whose experience is comparable to, or a bit ahead of, her own. Those who choose a historical figure, as she did, may have a sentimental streak, but in her case it may be more a matter of finding someone whose life embodied the leadership qualities she admires. If this exec/philanthropist hadn't named anyone famous in her test, that might have indicated that she is especially humanistic, kind, and humble. Not everyone wants to be out there in front.

The many references to sophisticated society, coupled with her answer about the cousin she feels close to, tell me that she likes the comfort of being with people in her peer group whom she doesn't have to explain things to. She wins the jackpot for not being able to answer number 4; it's good that she would prefer to be herself. People who can answer this question are usually thinking of the lifestyle or some aspect of another person's life rather than the whole person. I might think of a beautiful actress, but I don't really want to stop being myself and enter her life. I'd probably want to have a body like hers and keep my intelligence. Most people respond to this question with their senses—they don't want to give up their souls. The executive's realistic attitude about her life tells me that she's a positive person who makes the most of what she has.

Question number 5 can sometimes tell me about a client's mental state. Balanced people tend to choose a place that's comparable to where they already live so that they could fit in there. It's hard to live outside your sphere of influence. Paris offers many of the same pleasures and cultural advantages the executive enjoys in New York; she is not a small-town person. Test takers who choose an island might want to escape from their lives. Those who choose a country with an extremely foreign culture could have a simple case of wanderlust, or something more serious—a genuine disaffection with the environment. This was the case with two male clients I knew who never put anything in their desks or hung anything on the walls of their offices because they had no intention of getting comfortable and staying put. The office was a place to hang their hats and move on. What they didn't realize was that their behavior caused their colleagues to think of them as passing through. Their peers saw no reason for loyalty.

Question 6 is interesting because our neuroses drive many of our positive and negative behaviors, and looking at an emotional trauma from childhood is one way to zero in. Some people can't get beyond events from the past, and if they come from a painful beginning, they often go back to pain because it's familiar. But it isn't what happens to people that molds them, it's what they do with what happens that counts. The painful memory can tell you what to avoid in your later life, and as you examine it, ask yourself if you're still reacting against it or if you've moved beyond it.

That goes for the good memory as well. We all know the former prom queen who can't outgrow that image and keeps the same hairstyle and makeup from the period of time during which she was popular. Then there's the man who can't leave behind the glory days when he quarterbacked the high school football team and enjoyed the hero worship of his classmates; he needs to shift into a more intellectual realm.

The executive's answers indicate how important it is to her to feel that she's outstanding in some way, and that the people in her life are loyal to her. Another answer might reveal that you value overcoming an obstacle or being disciplined. Knowing what rewards you is a great way to focus your energies toward getting more of it. The compliments the client selected tell me she's a balanced thinker who keeps a cool head as she analyzes information, while at the same time she is able to maintain her humanitarian feelings for others.

THE WINDFALL TEST

The Windfall Test can tell me whether a client's values are in line with the business role he or she has chosen. To find out how your values stack up, pretend you had the good fortune to win the lottery.

1. How will it change your life?
2. In what ways will your life remain the same?
3. How will it affect your lifestyle?
4. How will you share the wealth?
5. Who else will this affect?

Aside from showing how willing someone is to be generous, this test is another means of comparing someone's current situation to his values. The answers can really cut to the heart of what bothers him about his life; one client said he'd tell off his boss, another would dump his girlfriend, another would buy his company and fire his manager, and another would leave town.

Even more interesting to me is whether people would use the money not so much to do more but to buy themselves out of their commitments. They might donate money to charities in place of volunteering time. It's easy to be impressed by the charitable donations of the affluent, but time is also a precious gift to give—rich or poor.

SELF-CONFIDENCE

First and foremost, self-confidence comes from knowing yourself better than anyone else does—and after taking a long, hard look, accepting what's there before deciding to make any changes. It means having enough self-esteem to never allow another person to exploit your strengths or your weaknesses—only you should control your own destiny. I believe that the following characteristics are essential if you are to reach your potential.

Ego Strength. The courage and fortitude to stay true to yourself under all circumstances—believing in your self-worth in the face of someone else's value judgment—even when it's rejection.

Ego Drive. The confidence to persuade another person to allow you to have your own way. It's the willpower necessary to go for personal gratification at the expense of someone else. For those on a "power trip" there's no sweeter reward for the psyche.

Empathy. The ability to blend individual values and drives with the needs of others. It is the humanistic side of life that goes beyond oneself. It's the powerful tool with which to persuade!

THE TRUTH OR DARE TEST

Have you ever wondered how others respond to you? It's easy to find out by asking several different people in your life: a personal friend; a family member; a social acquaintance; and a business associate, competitor, or superior.

Be brave. Offer anonymity to the people you're asking so they'll be honest with you. When you put your name on each test, code the forms by writing your name differently on each form. When the tests come back, you can evaluate and weigh the importance of each response. Have them grade you on the strength of the qualities listed below, using a scale of A, B, or C. A = Very strong, B = Average, C = Weak.

SOCIAL IMPRESSIONS

	A	B	C
Flexible			
Versatile			
Trustworthy			
Reliable			
Cooperative			
Competitive			
Risk taker			
Aggressive			
Supportive			
Dynamic			
Argumentative			
Questioner			
Copes with stress			
Sense of justice			

People-oriented			
Assertive			
Tough-minded			
Loyal			
Independent			
NAME			

You'll undoubtedly discover that you don't always come across the way you'd like to think you do. No one does. Reading the results of this test takes a good measure of ego strength—one of the three essential qualities discussed above.

Keep a cool head and maintain your self-confidence as you read your ratings and think of the advantage you've gained. Everyone sizes up everyone else, and now you know not only what the checklist is but also how you score. Some observers may also have figured out your blind spot—the aspect of your personality or packaging that is holding you back. They're not going to pull you aside and tell you what it is—the way I do with my clients—but your success hinges on identifying it and minimizing it.

The Truth or Dare Test, along with the values tests, help you to recognize that blind spot. Once you know what was previously unknown to you, you are in control of almost every aspect of the impression you make and you can modify it to suit any occasion. And still be your own person.

The consequences of disregarding your blind spot can be serious, as in the following story.

Case Study: Lois, 51

Lois was a self-made accounting executive in museum administration who'd climbed to the number-two spot. She hired me to be her Dutch uncle and help her make the leap into the top job.

I recognized from the results of her tests that Lois perversely enjoyed *struggling.* She had immigrated to the United States as a child and took great pride in her Old World heritage and self-sacrificing ways. All she ever did was complain, and her outlook was so negative that colleagues would run for cover whenever they saw her coming down the hall. She was a walking litany of her misfortunes, chewing on every painful detail of the day's conflicts with relish. At every opportunity she swelled with pride as she expounded on the problems she was able to overcome.

After we had worked together for a time, Lois became aware of her shortcomings. The tests revealed that she thought it was actually insincere to be cordial to everyone; indeed, Lois wasn't even pleasant. Her negative attitude stemmed from her strict childhood home; she had been reprimanded to the point where she was constantly trying to improve. She carried that role into her daily life, criticizing others in a misguided effort to motivate them to do better. Encouraging them with positive comments had never occurred to her.

I helped her see that she was putting all her eggs in one basket by depending solely on her number-crunching skill for recognition. If she worked on her appearance and attitude, Lois could attract people to her rather than chasing them away.

Prior to a board of directors meeting at which Lois was scheduled to make a presentation, I took her for a day of shopping and repackaged her from top to toe: hairstyle, makeup, designer wardrobe. Her salary was adequate to afford these luxuries, but having them didn't jibe with her self-sacrificing ways. In fact, she returned all of the purchases the next day. She traded a silk blouse for polyester wash-and-wear; Ferragamo pumps for cheap copies; a black wool Donna Karan suit for a poorly cut no-name imitation.

At the board of directors meeting Lois looked inappropriate. She hardly fitted the role of a boss-in-waiting and made a poor impression. Soon afterward, she was forced out of her job. Disciplined as she was at work, Lois couldn't apply the same discipline to adjusting her *values* to match her aspirations. Her goals required more than financial expertise, they required finesse—something Lois did not, and could not, *value*.

THREE-SECOND OVERVIEW

After evaluating your values, you may find you're limiting your opportunities to blend with those whom you admire and with whom you aspire to identify. This doesn't require changing your fine ethics or morals. It just means expanding your point of view.

The next chapter will continue to bring you new insights through some tests that will pinpoint your personality and communicating style.

3

Your Personality DNA

SELF-AWARENESS: POWER SECRET #2

This humble-pie, standing-in-the-shadows demeanor is nonsense—you needn't be reticent about the talent you've been given to deliver; you're just the messenger. It's your obligation to share it with the world, and it's easy to do when you learn to be an unabashed self-promoter. Like any good salesperson, it behooves you to know your product and believe in it. Self-awareness will build confidence in your unique talent and it will prevent critics from controlling you, the negative criticisms you've lived with will no longer deter you, you will be able to share your gifts with pride and joy.

In this chapter there are tests that will define your personality—the driving force behind your talent. As Henry Kissinger once said, history is fueled not by impersonal forces, but by personalities. If yours is out of sync, it may need some work. That doesn't mean adopting a phony persona, it simply means adjusting your communicating style in order to be more effective.

There are a lot of personality tests out there with one thing in common: they help you figure out who you are so you can understand your psyche and be at peace with it. I believe adopting that approach means missing out on an opportunity. If your test score shows that you're an introvert, your shyness may be holding you back. Why not attempt to overcome it by sharing your talent?

Understanding your own personality makes it easier to analyze anyone else with whom you come into contact—without giving them any tests. It takes only three seconds to figure out if someone is an extrovert or an introvert, creative or commonsensical, factual or emotional, judgmental or open-minded. You may say to yourself: "I don't know the boss (or whomever) well enough to analyze him." My response is, yes, you do. There are simple signs that signal personality types, and I'll teach you how to recognize them, even in strangers.

When people who work together have opposing personality types, they can spend as much time trying to overcome their different styles as they do accomplishing something of value. Those who are too practical never seem to get along with those who are creative. Many careers are needlessly derailed by such conflicts, so I advise people to know themselves and accept others.

PERSONALITY RESEARCH

Carl Gustav Jung, the famous Swiss psychiatrist (1875–1961), felt that people's choices are determined by their personality traits. He theorized that people generally fall into four basic communicating styles: intuitor, thinker, feeler, or senser. He observed that "People have a balance of styles, a primary style and a backup style; it's the interaction that determines their total approach to the world." For more on his theories, I suggest *Please Understand Me,* a book by David Keirsey and Marilyn Bates, clinical psychologists.

PINPOINT YOUR PERSONALITY

We are all a combination of many personality traits and that combination determines the way we think, feel, and behave—all the qualities that influence the unique style with which we express ourselves. Generally, most people have a stronger affinity for one of these communicating styles than the others. Or you may even be one of those rarely gifted individuals who are evenly endowed in every style.

In business, each of the four basic personality styles has merit, so in this chapter, I will help you discover which of the following primary styles suits your temperament.

Leader—determines a mission, sets goals, and leads
Initiator—conceives or develops a service or product
Administrator—coordinates the manpower effort
Salesman—sells a service or product

Before you try to pinpoint your distinctive style, you need to take the following test for a comprehensive overview of the personal characteristics, communicating style, and biases you bring to the working world—and how the balance may be affecting your progress at work. Many corporations give their managerial candidates similar tests. You certainly don't want your company to know more about your psychological profile than you do!

BUSINESS PERSONALITY PROFILE

1. If I were invited to make a major business speech, I'd be
   (a) stimulated by the opportunity
   (b) less than thrilled at speaking before a crowd
2. When I interview a prospective new employee, I seek someone who is
   (a) sensible and results-oriented
   (b) a creative problem solver
3. I prefer to
   (a) play by the rules, within an established system
   (b) find new ways to approach a problem
4. Persuading another person requires that I
   (a) offer pertinent information that will influence their decision
   (b) make them feel important to the activity
5. In resolving a controversy, I am persuaded by
   (a) the reasons for the conflict
   (b) fear of emotional repercussions
6. I recognize the importance of
   (a) planning my schedule carefully
   (b) being flexible with my time

7. When investing in the market, I
   (a) evaluate a stock's performance carefully
   (b) sometimes take a risk and buy on impulse
8. My response to an unexpected meeting is one of
   (a) curiosity about the reason for the meeting
   (b) dismay at being interrupted
9. I'd rather work in a
   (a) large bank
   (b) design studio
10. Computers are essential for business primarily because they
    (a) are timesavers
    (b) have limitless uses
11. Organizations value executives for their
    (a) analytical ability
    (b) loyalty to the team
12. Today's politicians and business leaders need to be more
    (a) ethical
    (b) compassionate
13. At important group meetings, I'm more likely to
    (a) decide which criteria should be followed
    (b) encourage candid participation
14. Some business deals take time to close, but I remain
    (a) tenacious
    (b) patient and easygoing
15. When a business contact calls me, I usually
    (a) accept the call
    (b) have a secretary or machine screen the call to avoid inter-
    ruptions
16. I'm endowed with
    (a) a good dose of common sense
    (b) a creative flair
17. Friends and associates have told me that I am
    (a) too practical and lack imagination
    (b) not down-to-earth enough
18. In a crisis, I usually become
    (a) cool and logical
    (b) emotional and less composed

19. I try never to
    (a) leave things to chance so there can be no mistakes
    (b) find fault because everyone makes mistakes

20. It frustrates me when a manager
    (a) delays making a decision
    (b) jumps to conclusions

21. I usually plan my schedule
    (a) well in advance
    (b) to be flexible enough for spur-of-the-moment events

22. At the office, when peers are working on a project
    (a) I wonder what they are involved in
    (b) I concentrate on my own business

23. As an occupation, I am better suited for
    (a) sales and marketing
    (b) research and development

24. Managing people requires empathy, but I find it's challenging to
    (a) relate to them
    (b) solve their problems

25. Corporations that are most successful
    (a) plan long term to achieve their objectives
    (b) build and retain a harmonious organization

26. It is a splendid trait to
    (a) have organizational skills
    (b) be creative and open to new ideas

27. Executives who succeed are
    (a) decision makers
    (b) flexible

28. Reviewing an assignment that failed, I realize that
    (a) I goofed and feel guilty about the outcome
    (b) I gave it my best effort and move forward

29. I prefer a job where I have contact with
    (a) a wide variety of people
    (b) a limited number of associates

30. I prefer working with people who regard street smarts as
    (a) invaluable in making decisions
    (b) unprofessional and unreliable for decisions

31. As a weekend guest at a friend's home, I help
   (a) when directed what to do
   (b) by trying to find something that needs to be done

32. When something goes awry, before I draw a conclusion,
   (a) I study the circumstances very carefully
   (b) I try to get a feel for what happened

33. One of my assets is the ability to be
   (a) cautious until all of the facts are in
   (b) trusting of other individuals

34. It is my desire never to work for anyone who is
   (a) unreasonably prejudiced or who plays favorites
   (b) ruthless and unfeeling

35. The best meetings I attend
   (a) are well organized and have an agenda
   (b) encourage brainstorming

36. Calling on potential clients is
   (a) interesting and enjoyable
   (b) time-consuming and enervating

37. A new computer is probably easier to
   (a) produce
   (b) design

38. When I go to a movie, I enjoy a plot that
   (a) has a strong message
   (b) stimulates my imagination

39. Contemporaries probably say that I am capable of being
   (a) sarcastic and unfeeling at times
   (b) too sensitive to criticism

40. I avoid business associates who are
   (a) hotheaded
   (b) dispassionate

41. Business deals are better with
   (a) a formal contract
   (b) a gentlemen's agreement

42. I'd rather go to the airport
   (a) early to allow for any check-in problems
   (b) just before take-off time

43. At a controversial meeting, I'd put in my two cents with

    (a) ease, if I thought it were important
    (b) difficulty, because it wouldn't help the situation

44. Philosophically, each day brings me
    (a) pleasure
    (b) closer to my dreams

45. When purchasing something new, I look for styling that is
    (a) classic and long-lasting
    (b) fashionable and in vogue

46. If I had to challenge a tax audit, I'd prefer to
    (a) research my records and provide proof
    (b) arrange a settlement to avoid the emotional strain

47. Once I commit to a challenge, I remain
    (a) steadfast in reaching my goal
    (b) loyal to everyone who is dedicated to the cause

48. In negotiations, I want
    (a) an offer on the table
    (b) open bidding, so I can continue to bargain

49. If someone unexpectedly comes into my office it is usually
    (a) uncluttered and orderly
    (b) messy and disorganized

50. Being promoted or starting a new assignment
    (a) is an interesting challenge
    (b) puts me under a heavy strain

51. Sometimes I accept life
    (a) the way it is and go along with it
    (b) as a challenge and look forward to the next stage

52. I read newspaper columnists who
    (a) report straight news
    (b) comment satirically on current events

53. The business environment would be better if people
    (a) were more concerned about the environment
    (b) were more concerned about poverty

54. When something upsetting happens to me, I
    (a) keep it to myself and try to work it out
    (b) share my feelings with a close friend

55. Customers expect me to approach them
    (a) with an agenda or plan

(b) with an open mind ready to brainstorm

56. It's easier for others to find a solution
    (a) if they know how to follow the rules
    (b) if they have no preconceived notions

57. Business associates probably describe me as
    (a) approachable and friendly
    (b) rather reserved and aloof

58. My daily routine is appealing because
    (a) there are no surprises
    (b) no two days are alike

59. Training directors should stress
    (a) the ABCs of serving customers
    (b) problem solving and innovative thinking

60. I take pride in my
    (a) intelligence and education
    (b) compassion and generosity

61. At retirement parties, people become
    (a) thoughtful about the significance of the occasion
    (b) sentimental and soft-hearted

62. My adrenaline flows when I
    (a) finalize a deal
    (b) am in the middle of competitive bidding

63. If the truth were known, I'm really
    (a) conventional and traditional
    (b) impulsive and a nonconformist

64. On vacation, I prefer to spend time
    (a) with a group—at a resort or on a tour
    (b) alone—reading, visiting museums, or sightseeing

65. In editorials written about controversial topics, I prefer
    (a) an analysis of the problem
    (b) proposals for solving the problem

66. The books I prefer to read are mostly
    (a) nonfiction
    (b) fiction

67. It's politically wise to recognize the opportune time to
    (a) express my opinion
    (b) reserve comment

68. When an employee makes an error, it is better to be
    (a) firm about correcting the problem
    (b) understanding and considerate
69. Involvement in a project brings me a sense of satisfaction
    (a) upon completion
    (b) during the process
70. Preparing for an important meeting, I work better
    (a) against a deadline
    (b) at my own pace

SCORING

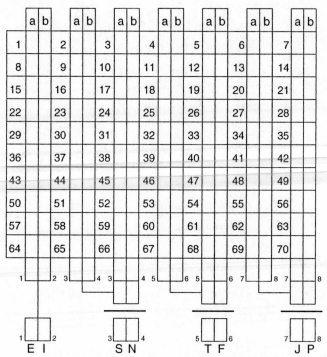

Enter your answers with a check in column A or B. Add every column down to the numbered boxes and follow the arrows to transfer your scores as shown. Get your final score by totaling the columns in the lettered boxes.

E = Extrovert (gregarious)   I = Introvert (solitary)
S = Senser (sensible)   N = Intuitor (ingenious)
T = Thinker (analytical)   F = Feeler (persuasive)
J = Judgmental (decisive)   P = Perceptive (tentative)

Generally, you will find that in each letter combination, such as
E versus I, one score is higher than the other. Write down the letter
corresponding to the higher score in each of these pairings and
you'll have your "type"; an example would be INFP, or ESTJ.

For further information about your type—style or traits—match
the letters from your test with those on the following chart:

BASIC PERSONALITY PROFILES

*SP (ISTP, ESTP, ISFP, ESFP) = a person with a sense of
"entitlement"*
Independent, free-spirited, risk taker, impulsive, energetic, generous, fickle, affectionate, lives in the present
*SJ (ISFJ, ESFJ, ISTJ, ESTJ) = a person who believes in the
"work ethic"*
Conservative, traditionalist, comfortable in hierarchical structure,
honor bound and obligated, pessimist, joiner, backbone of society
*NT (INTP, ENTP, INTF, ENTJ) = a person who tends to
"focus on the future"*
Creative thinker, inquisitive, competent perfectionist, self-criti-
cal, terse, capable of sarcasm, candid, usually open-minded
*NF (INFJ, ENFJ, INFP, ENFP) = a person who wants a
"unique identity"*
Genuine, enthusiastic, intellectual butterfly, inspires, fluent
speaker and writer, people watcher, empathetic, sees potential
good in everyone

It may be entertaining to decipher your personality DNA, but
that's only part of the game. Now you need to see how well balanced
you are. To do this, I want you to envision yourself as an automobile
driven by your personality—your brain is the powerful engine and
each wheel represents one personality trait that will help you move

forward if all four wheels are in balance. In case of a significant imbalance, you may need to supplement your weakness with a "spare tire." For example, an Intuitor (innovator) would bring in a Senser (salesperson) to take care of marketing. A Thinker (leader) would not survive long without a Feeler (administrator).

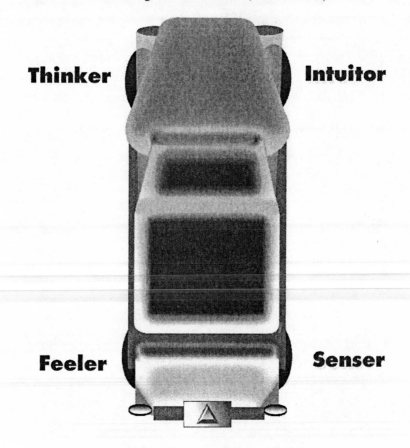

Thinker

Intuitor

Feeler

Senser

There are two additional components which influence your personality and perspective—your power source and your call to action.

Imagine the power source as fuel for your engine, and the call to action as the journey. A person who is an introvert draws on fuel from within. The extrovert is fueled by external forces.

The basis for moving ahead is determined by whether you are the judgmental type who focuses on your destination, decides how to get there, follows the plan, and arrives on schedule, or whether you are the more open-minded, perceptive type, who likes the flexibility to leave your options open.

To determine the balance you bring to the game, it's necessary to transfer the numbers from the test scores to the corresponding areas on the automobile.

If you are mature and empathetic, you'll be well equipped to move ahead at optimum speed. However, if you are soft in some areas, the imbalance will slow you down. I've found the easy way to correct that deficit is by broadening your perspective to understand more than one point of view. Let's start by learning to understand each other.

PERSONALITY DIFFERENCES

Introvert (I) versus Extrovert (E). Introverts are deep thinkers who prefer time alone to read or stare at their computer screens or gaze into outer space. Reflective, quiet, and knowledgeable, they strive for and appreciate excellence. Contrary to stereotype, introverts often have rich friendships. These are their positive qualities. But, as with all personality types, there are negative potentials to being an introvert, and it is these negatives that each type must be aware of and possibly seek to change. For the introvert, they include a tendency to be suspicious and worried. Introverts can also be intellectual snobs who are unaccepting of others and perfectionists to a fault. They may be self-centered and have jealous friendships.

Much of introversion is caused by shyness and lack of experience. Of all the personality traits, I think that introversion is the one characteristic that most needs to be remedied. Why? Introversion borders on selfishness. By hanging back during interactions with others, introverts are protecting themselves, even feeding their own egos. A conversation is like a rowboat that requires the exertion of both participants to keep moving forward; an introvert isn't engaging his oar. It shouldn't be the other person's job to row the boat for both, should it? The introvert must help. If it means fighting his shy impulses in order to be outgoing and kind to other people, so be it. In both office and social interactions, it's everyone's job to contribute to relationships and make others comfortable.

Extroverts aren't perfect, but our society tends to reward their behavior, especially in business and social life. They have many good qualities, including their friendliness and magnetism. Energetic and sparkling, they inspire others. They like people, variety, and action, and are easy to talk to. The extrovert likes to chat a lot, to walk around the halls asking everybody how they are. Not that they want to know the honest answer, mind you, they're just looking for a reaction. They get their energy from other people. You won't see an extrovert going to the movies alone, eating dinner alone, taking a vacation alone. Extroverts are born leaders who know how important it is to kiss the babies. It should come as no surprise that most CEOs and politicians are extroverts.

Still, extroverts can be hyperactive, intrusive, and brash. They need to be the center of attention at times and have a habit of boasting. Paradoxically, this is sometimes because they don't tap into their own reservoir of strength and thus haven't learned their own value. They're looking for a vote of confidence from the outside, even if they have to solicit it.

Here's an example: One night I was at an elegant party at a private club. Eight of us were dressed in our silk-and-satin finest and seated at a magnificent table with a striking floral centerpiece. One woman monopolized the conversation. She talked on and on about her vacation and wouldn't yield the floor. Finally I suggested she had chosen such a great topic that we should go around the table and each tell a story about a vacation. Unchastened, the woman tried to interrupt several times; each person's story prompted a "me too" anecdote from her. Several people gently reminded that she had to wait until it was her turn to speak again. She was an extrovert out of control—not willing to share the limelight. Paradoxically, she was behaving like an introvert who resists building links with others.

Drawing attention to oneself can be a narcissistic, "me too" trap for both introverts and extroverts. Have you ever told someone how you broke your leg, only to hear about the time the person cracked a tibia skiing? We've all been guilty of it, and it's yet another example of why you shouldn't feel threatened to contemplate balancing your personality as a result of your test score. It can mean becoming a better person, not a different one.

The easiest way to achieve rapport with others is to make them feel that you're interested in sharing their contribution to the conversation. Remember, time together is either a learning or entertaining experience. It's easy to draw people into any dialogue by inviting them to add a comment or an opinion. I tell my clients to "share the pie" with everyone present. It's the diplomatic way to acknowledge them with a slice of time. You'll make more points if you don't drain other people's energy by dominating or shortchanging the conversation.

Your score may indicate that you straddle the line between these two types, neither a clear introvert nor an extrovert. If so, you might spot parts of yourself in descriptions of both types. That's good, and here's why: balance. A balanced personality can unlock doors for you and give you the resources to be comfortable in any situation, with any person.

As you saw in your test score, introvert versus extrovert is just one piece of the personality type puzzle. The next pair to focus on is senser versus intuitor.

Senser (S) versus Intuitor (N). The word "senser" doesn't always mean exactly what it seems to say. It sounds close to "feeler," part of one of the other pairs of attributes, but it's quite the opposite. A senser is a just-the-facts person, and he gets that way by using his objective senses, rather than his intuition, to gather information. A senser relies on his eyes, ears, and body to clue him in. Practical and bottom-line oriented, sensers are doers who want action and want it now. They are competitive and fall into two categories of achievement: either perfectionists or discoverers. Perfectionists work on something and make it better, whereas discoverers go beyond the norm and look for new or better ways. Both are highly organized and set high standards for themselves.

Sensers are master manipulators who can fiddle with the senses of others. This can translate into an ability to make money, and in my work I've observed that a high sensing score generally goes hand in hand with high compensation. Such people have a talent for eliciting the response they want from people; many actors and comedians are sensers for just that reason. In business, sensers make their bosses happy by bringing in the profits. When it comes to appearance, they prefer to wear comfortable, functional clothing, but peer pressure means so much to them that a male senser will give in to the current vogue and wear suspenders with his suits if that's what everyone he admires is wearing.

The negative aspects of sensers come from their constant need to feed and gratify their own senses. They can be self-involved, arrogant, and status-seeking. Manipulating people can become an end in itself, turning an unethical senser into a snake oil salesman. Sensers tend to act first and think later. Sometimes they have trouble seeing long range, overlooking important steps in the planning process. They can be domineering and lacking in trust. A senser boss can become frustrated with touchy-feely underlings, over-supervising them or snatching work away from them in the belief that the only way to get something done right is to do it himself.

The intuitor trait is identified by the letter N to differentiate it from the letter I for introvert. Just a scant 10% of the population falls into the category of intuitor (N), so you're dealing with a rare bird. Albert Einstein is the classic intuitor: a genius who didn't speak until he was six years old. Intuitors gather information through a sort of osmosis, absorbing ESP signals and cosmic energy. Creative, imaginative, and original, they are driven by inspiration and a powerful intellect. Intuitors see the big picture in spite of a tenuous grasp of the details. They anticipate rather than validate. Folks with this trait can be quite charismatic, although they tend to be unaware of their effect on people. Intuitors are magnets to each other, finding their counterparts in the arts, sciences, wherever— but always on the cutting edge. Their nonconformity makes them dress in unusual combinations. In fact, they'll wear anything, and the effect is more often beautiful than trendy.

On the other hand, intuitors can drive others to madness, especially in the workplace. At times they're unrealistic and impractical. They're allergic to focusing on details and dislike documenting their work process. Fantasy-bound, they can be long on vision and short on action. Intuitors are often dogmatic, becoming impatient with people who don't take their conclusions seriously—which can seem abrasive to more practical members of management.

Thinker (T) versus Feeler (F). Talk about the mainstay of society—thinkers make the world run smoothly. They make life better for everyone because of their strong work ethic and high standards. The sort of information process they follow is robotic: they either start at the bottom and go up, or they begin with some product or challenge and break it down. Deliberate, prudent, and objective, thinkers dwell in the world of rationality and analysis. Thinkers like to sleep on it. Many are effective communicators, possibly because they consider carefully before they speak. They work in orderly offices with research books lining the walls. They make good jurors, who wait until closing arguments are concluded before weighing the evidence carefully. Their checkbooks are balanced.

Thinkers tend to like tailored, conservative clothing. They prefer ties and scarfs in precise patterns. If they're affluent, they've got a club tie indicating they met the rigid qualifications for entry to a top-ranked school. If they're less well off, they own something that signifies they belong to some kind of organization. You might assume that thinker versus feeler is a classic man-woman issue, but that's far too easy. Teaching, a profession chosen by as many women as men, is often favored by thinkers.

Thinkers can get trapped in their love of analysis, becoming overcautious and indecisive. They can frustrate feelers in relationships by being too rigid, impersonal, and unemotional. Some of them walk around with monster superiority complexes, trying at every turn to prove they're smarter than others. Some don't care how they look because they're trying to send a message: *I have too big a brain to concern myself with frivolities like appearance.* But they're not out to hurt anyone; they forget their own feelings as well as the feelings of others. Thinkers often forget to stop and smell the roses.

These cerebral types can sound like sticks-in-the-mud, but don't take them lightly. Some of the finest minds in the world fall into this category. Put this trait together with extroversion and you've got one hell of a leader. It's when a thinker is also an introvert that the two traits can pile negatively on top of one another. You can imagine an introvert-thinker tied hour after hour to her beloved computer, cloning chimpanzee DNA. Such a character would have a legitimate reason for isolating herself with her machine and would be in danger of losing her ability to adjust to other people.

Feelers operate from the heart and the gut. They're warm and touchy-feely. They're always observing interactions among people and interpreting them. *Why didn't she invite me to that meeting? Was that look he gave me a sign of disapproval?* Feelers read between the lines. They are nurturing and empathetic—the Mother Bears of the group. Their offices can be a mess of papers and coffee cups because they'd rather draw someone out than write a report or put things away. Their need for an emotional response can have an odd side effect: whatever childhood behavior got attention from their parents is the one they'll pursue in a modified form as adults. So a feeler kid who got strokes for bringing home straight A's turns into a feeler adult who works overtime at the office.

Feelers are not trendsetters; they are more comfortable in the mainstream, following traditional values. They like colorful clothes that reflect their emotions. They are loyal, spontaneous, and persuasive. But all is not hearts and flowers. Feelers overreact and get defensive if things don't go their way. Their need to psychoanalyze everything gets them into trouble as they over-personalize every interaction, stirring up conflict. Some are guilt-ridden, ruled by thoughts of what they've done wrong. In the office, feelers get tripped up by their tendency to be subjective, disregarding the facts in favor of instinct. Their delightful spontaneity can turn to impulsiveness, getting in the way of their work and causing them to postpone necessary chores.

Judge (J) versus Perceiver (P). People who take a "judging" attitude aren't any more judgmental than the rest of us. Any personality type can be judgmental. Instead, the J versus P scale tells you what approach you take to dealing with the outside world. J refers to people who like to draw conclusions and have things settled, whereas P refers to those who delay decision making and prefer to leave things open-ended.

If you are a judge, you like to think you have some control over life. Judges are structured and organized; they want to finish things and move along. They set standards for themselves and for others, and follow them. Judges are surprised every time someone fails to live up to their expectations, as if that were unusual. They set goals and meet them, thriving on the resulting sense of closure.

Perceivers are always receptive to more information or stimulation before acting. They take each day as it comes and don't kick themselves for letting chores slide into tomorrow. Perceivers generally grew up in either an unstructured environment or a very structured one against which they rebel as adults. These people can be very kind to others because they're kind to themselves. They don't whip up a storm because you're late or take offense if you ask them a personal question. They see life as a process. A lot of artistic people fall into this category.

Now that you've analyzed your personality let's do something with the information. You can use what you've learned in the following ways:

- *Achieve a more balanced personality.*
- *Recognize your strengths and capitalize on them.*
- *Identify your weaknesses and remedy them.*
- *Protect your vulnerabilities from manipulation by others.*

It takes a lot of self-discipline to apply what you have learned about your personality type but the following case history will show how a client was able to compensate for her weakness so she could move ahead.

She applied her awareness of her own personality profile in combination with that of her new boss to achieve her goals.

Case Study: Cindy, Age 35

This is the tale of a classic intuitor who learned how to compensate for her underdeveloped senser side—the component of her personality geared toward making money and finding career satisfaction. Cindy was a typical creative person, full of ideas but lacking an ability to think in terms of the bottom line. She was a poor negotiator who had little political sense. When she came to me for help, she was between jobs as a designer for companies such as Avon and the Franklin Mint.

We determined her needs: a well-paid, stable, design director's role in an established company. Cindy was pretty, Southern, and generous; she needed a position powerful enough to protect her from being manipulated by jealous coworkers who had eaten her for lunch each time she was the new kid on the block at her other companies. When we talked to recruiters and looked at the want ads to find a position to shoot for, we found an opening for a design director with a popularly priced china company whose biggest customer was a national discount retailer. The fact that this company was a bit below her level of sophistication would help her to create a mystique and get the perks we were looking for.

Before I let her interview for the job, I had to build her confidence. Confidence comes with expertise, so I called all my resources for information about china companies. I conducted my own market research by posing as a mother of the bride and asking store salespersons which patterns and colors were selling best. Knowing this data would make Cindy sound plugged-in to the customer. Because her previous Northeastern coworkers had hazed her about her Southern gentility, I instructed her to ask for a more senior position than the one that was advertised so that she would have hiring and firing responsibilities. After all, when you can threaten people's existence in a company, they're not going to menace you. I also instructed Cindy to ask for further perks, including market trips to Europe and Asia, a title of vice president, an office with a window, and veto power over sales force recommendations to modify her designs based on input from the field.

Cindy let out a yell and said: "You're crazy, I can't pull that off!" She was used to retreating into her identity of artiste, telling herself she didn't have it in her to fight for privileges, especially up front. But I explained that it was time she established a power base going into a company, rather than taking the role of martyr and leaving a company when she didn't get what she wanted. A woman usually gets a diamond ring before she walks down the aisle, not ten years into the marriage. The size of the diamond tells her something about the lifestyle she can expect with her future husband. That may be a cynical example, but it certainly applies to interviewing for jobs. The way a new employer treats you going in is very revealing. And although Cindy may not have felt her power, she had a lot of experience at profitable companies to offer, and she deserved to be compensated for it. Men often ask for a contract or golden parachute as a safety net.

Cindy took the gamble, and we giggled our way to her interview. I coached her to ask for the extras in stages. She had to work on the chairman to convince him to give her the market trips, but soon he caved in, and I told her that once he began to bend he'd keep bending. She asked for the VP title so she'd have stature with the media. Once the chairman approved that, she asked for hiring and firing privileges. After she started work, she told the company she needed an office with natural light for her designing, knowing full well that the only such room available was a large conference room. The company gave it to her on a provisional basis only, so I told her to take over the space, filling it with color charts and china samples and big trees. It worked—they never did kick her out of there. Don't laugh; the theory behind gaining physical space is in Machiavelli's *The Prince.*

Cindy's story illustrates the fact that you don't have to change your colors like a chameleon to tap into personality strengths you don't possess. True, Cindy pushed herself to make uncomfortably demanding requests. But once she finished negotiating, she had landed herself a job that allowed her to be herself and function without the distractions that had plagued her in the past.

Take a look at your scores again, and note which pairs of traits are more balanced and which are lopsided. Then decide how you want to address these imbalances. Do you lack a skill you've always wanted to develop, such as organization or friendliness? Is there something you can do to cultivate this trait? If so, set reasonable goals for change and give it a go. Remember that you don't have to transform yourself into another person; just add another maneuver to your bag of tricks. Any determined person can learn to negotiate like a head of state, even if he's not naturally aggressive.

But if you don't think you have it in you, you can do what Cindy did and hire a business adviser.

UNDERSTAND OTHERS: POWER SECRET #3

- Learn to read people.
- Strategically introduce your concepts by adapting to their style.
- Lead and inspire by incorporating others' personality styles.
- Survive politically in a competitive environment.

Whether or not you identify aspects of your persona you want to change, you can use personality typing to modify your approach to different people in your workplace or social circle. It's easy—just use what you know about that person to guess his or her personality type and identify areas where your type and his have trouble communicating. Then bridge the gap.

My clients are often skeptical when I tell them they have enough information to guess other people's personality types without using complicated tests. It's so simple *you don't even have to meet the person* in order to identify his defining personality traits. Here's proof. The managing partner of a prominent law firm invited me to visit him and gave me a tour of the facilities.

It was a Sunday, so the office was nearly deserted. The space was decorated with oriental rugs and original oil paintings that fought for attention with the million-dollar views. As we walked the halls, the attorney asked me for my impressions. We stopped at an office that was in a state of total disarray. I told him that its occupant took great pride in being smarter than everybody else. The overwhelming mess indicated he couldn't turn on a dime and was not innovative. He was probably inflexible, stubborn, and meanspirited when challenged. The partner asked, "How did you figure that out?"

"This office has no more paper on the floor than any other," I replied, "but every stack is going in a different direction, and there doesn't seem to be any pattern of organization. If other people have to work with this attorney they go nuts because they can never find anything. That's the way he maintains control over his domain and makes himself feel indispensable."

"You've hit this guy right on the head," the partner said.

We walked around the corner and stood in the doorway of a fairly neat office with no nameplate. "The occupant of this office is a woman who is very nurturing and at times a little emotional," I surmised. "The fact that her desk is so neat and orderly tells me she's generally able to stay on top of things. There are six empty flower vases on her window sill, indicating she's either had a special event recently like a signed deal or celebrated a birthday, or she's put the vases up there to remind herself to take them home because if it's out of sight it's out of mind." The partner smiled. "That's exactly what she does!"

Finally, we passed a secretary chewing gum and reading a magazine. "She's a temp," I whispered. He raised his eyebrows and winked.

Let's do another demonstration. Remembering the descriptions of the attributes of each personality trait, choose someone in the public eye and size him or her up. Say you thought of Nelson Mandela, the human rights leader. Is he an introvert or an extrovert? An extrovert, because he energizes himself by moving among masses of people. A senser or an intuitor? Clearly the latter; he sees new ways to lead his people toward democracy and employs collective bargaining to persuade South Africa's powerful white minority to accept his policies. Thinker or feeler? Mandela is a strategist who travels the world to gather information to use at home—his brain rather than his emotions guides his actions. A judge or a perceiver? He sets standards for himself and meets them, always staying on target, never waffling. Talk about a planner—he sat in jail for *twenty-seven years* in the name of his cause. Thus: ENTJ. This is an interesting assessment, because ENTJ is the most common personality type for leaders, CEOs, and other public figures. Napoleon was an ENTJ.

This is a really easy one: Thomas Edison. He was an introverted genius with a brilliant open mind (INTP). Like Edison, most INTPs are drawn to science, research, and engineering. Colin Powell? He strikes me as an introvert who nonetheless manages to function well in a high-profile position. His senser abilities came in handy in a military emergency when he had to sell a course of action to the President and the American people. Although I'll call him a senser, I think those traits are balanced by intuition; Powell succeeded partly by formulating innovative war plans. He is a clear thinker and judge—he gathers objective facts, processes them linearly, and draws conclusions. ISTJ, in fact, is the personality type of most people who enter the military. It's also the profile of many police officers, administrators, and accountants.

You can even assess fictional characters. Jerry Seinfeld's sitcom alter ego? An introvert/extrovert, but the fact that he's a comedian makes the extroverted side win. Definite senser—most comedians and actors are. A thinker who is constantly embarrassed by the feeler girlfriends he tends to attract. Another balanced pair are his judge and perceiver traits, but I'll say perceiver because his mockery of nonsensical assumptions people take for granted provides the material for his comedy act. The diagnosis? ESTP, the personality type of many creative executives, entrepreneurs, and performing artists.

If you're trying to assign a personality type to someone you want to persuade in the workplace, such as your boss, gather extra information from coworkers and take a peek in your manager's office. Think about her clothing, manner, career track. Then use these questions to make your best guess.

What is her basis of power? Does she draw on others for her energy (E), or does she look within (I)?

How does she gather information? Objectively via her senses (S) or subjectively, from inspiration (N)?

What is her basis for making decisions? Thorough logical thought (T), or from a gut feeling (F)?

What is her basis for action? Is she trying to control her environment (J) or simply understand it (P)?

CUSTOMIZE YOUR APPROACH

Once you've figured out what makes your boss (or client, or colleague) tick, you have to decide what to do with that information.

You're not going to redesign your personality to suit your boss's preferences. He may be a senser, but that doesn't mean he can't appreciate the creative people working for him. He knows he needs their expertise. It's more a question of communication—if you're one of his creative staff, how are you going to speak his language? How are you going to get what you want or need from him?

Decide which traits are getting in the way of good communication between the two of you. (Is the problem that you're creative and he's bottom-line oriented? Or is it that he's outgoing and you're shy?) Then modify your presentation accordingly.

Approach an Extrovert. Here's a case where sharing a trait with the person you're trying to reach can be an obstacle. Lock two extroverts in a room and each will complain that the other is a poor conversationalist. (An extrovert thinks a good conversationalist is someone who is interested in what *he* has to say.) So if you're an extrovert too, be aware of rank and allow your superior to take the floor. Ask questions to draw him out. If you're an introvert, try to seem a bit bolder, a bit more comfortable in your own skin. Appear interested in what your boss has to say, and when it's your turn to speak, keep it simple, direct, and animated. Extroverts are easily bored by topics that aren't directly related to them.

Approach an Introvert. If you're an introvert, you must allow for the other person's introversion. Don't force your personality on him. Keep conversation to a minimum, and don't get personal—introverts don't like it. Let him dictate the pace, the volume, and the content of your interaction. Many introverts are simply shy or inexperienced, so if I need to work with one I allow our level of familiarity to progress at a slower pace and give him extra time to warm up to me.

Approach a Senser. You want to get the attention of a senser? Tell him what's in it for him. Describe how the project you want to control, or the assistant you want to hire, will make *him* a success. You can make almost any request sound like a gift to a results-hungry senser. I had a client I'll call Lucy who was overdue for a promotion from a supervisor who was under pressure from the company bigwigs to cut the fat from his department. Not the best atmosphere in which to make demands, right? I suggested that my client frame her request for a promotion as a way to *help* her supervisor rein in expenses. Lucy approached her boss and told him that there were three reasons why her promotion was in his best interests. First, she said, a colleague with the title she wanted had recently left the company, so the boss wouldn't have to create a new position for her. Second, the promotion would not change her function within the company, because she had taken on the responsibilities that went with the higher title the year before. Lucy then gave him documents to support her claim that she was already doing the new job. Third, Lucy explained, her promotion would *save* the company money, because once she had the new title she wouldn't be eligible for the pricey overtime she received for every hour she worked past 5 P.M. Lucy got her promotion, and as she predicted, it did cost her money; her raise was only half as much as her usual overtime pay. But the title heightened her prestige level and gave her a measure of tenure at the company.

Sometimes you will be thrown off by a senser's easygoing manner because of his sense of humor, but don't waste his time building your case. Get to the point quickly; remember that he's action-oriented and looking for short-term personal gain. If you walk into his office without any previous knowledge about his temperament, take a look around for clues. A senser decorates his walls and bookshelves with personal trophies and memorabilia that remind him of his conquests.

You will lose points if you ever try to upstage a senser. This type, of all of the others, wants to be the center of interest, as indicated by all of the personal trophies on his walls. The following case demonstrates how one conflict of personalities was resolved to the satisfaction of all concerned.

Case Study: Joe, 48

I got a call from a director at a chemical company asking me to work with an executive who'd been with the firm since it was founded. This executive's level of sophistication had not increased as the company expanded. In meetings, Joe put in his two cents at the wrong time or threw cold water on the chairman's ideas, embarrassing him in front of other executives. The chairman, a more cultured man who enjoyed his new upper-class status, was about ready to give Joe the boot. The chairman's attitude mystified Joe; he remembered the old days when they brainstormed together in a back office and took pride in their working-class roots.

After giving Joe my personality tests and having his handwriting analyzed, I discerned that he was a decent, quick-thinking intuitor who based all of his management skills on problem-solving. The chairman's governing trait was that of a senser who had a need to sell, an extrovert who liked to play to an audience to get positive reactions from others. This is a classic problem of mismatched personality types that Joe could overcome by learning how to communicate in the chairman's style.

Aside from the issues of class and appearance, Joe needed to appeal to his boss's emotions in order to get his information heard and appreciated. I explained to him that the boss's point of view was primarily solution-oriented.

Joe had failed to recognize the boss's entitlement. The one lesson everyone has to learn is, *the person who pays your rent deserves deference.* So I instructed Joe to pull his boss aside before a meeting to voice his preferences, and not to express his point of view in front of other people unless the chairman asked for it. True, there was a day when they had made plans together in a cubicle, but now they were in a boardroom, and the dynamics had changed.

Joe picked up the strategy in a flash. After we had worked together for just a day, Joe learned how to take care of his boss's ego. I explained to him that, since his mind worked faster than others', he had to restrain himself from blurting out the answer to every question like a hyperactive schoolboy. I suggested a game for him to play to cure the problem. He had to count how much more time it took other people to come up with the answer than it took him. Sometimes it took a count of 20, and Joe found that keeping score occupied his mind while he waited for his colleagues to catch up.

As Joe polished his presentation skills, he also updated his clothing, manner, and office décor in order to reach the sophistication level of his successful company. Joe was still Joe—but more confident and better accepted by his peers and superiors. Changing his appearance and manner didn't make him bitter. What he did wasn't tantamount to dumbing himself down, or changing his personality. He is still an innovator, and quick to come up with a solution. He just learned to hold his tongue and to package, present, and sell the strategies being churned out by his vector brain. He also learned how to respect other people's thinking processes. That's all.

Approach an Intuitor. Spark her curiosity. When I'm picking the brain of an intuitor, I ask her to problem-solve without judgments. I make it clear that she should free-associate without following any rules or routines. I want to hear her unedited ideas. It's always a good idea to give an intuitor a thinking space with windows, mirrors, glass—anything that's reflective. Award an intuitor on your team with a crystal paperweight.

If you're trying to impress an intuitor, don't waste time. You'll lose her attention if you give her a lot of background before you propose your Big Idea. Instead, respect her right-brain ability to jump to the heart of the matter in a flash, and appeal to her artistic sense by wearing an unusual watch or a whimsical pin.

Approach a Thinker. Overcoming the differences between a thinker and a feeler is easy to explain and tough to execute. When pitching an idea to a thinker, keep your interaction impersonal (as with an introvert) and stick to the facts. Do the opposite for a feeler—appeal to the person's emotions. The reason this is difficult is that after the first two or three sentences you may find yourself reverting back to your usual communication style, especially if the discussion becomes tense, as in a salary negotiation. Role-playing with someone who can help you stick to thinker or feeler lingo can help. When I'm trying to make an impression on a thinker, or reward him for a job well done, I give him a historical manuscript or beautiful first-edition book.

Prepare as well as you can for a meeting with a thinker. Everything in his office is organized, catalogued, and researched—he'll expect your presentation to be the same. More than any other personality type, the thinker will take in every detail of your ensemble in those precious three seconds after you walk in his door, so pay attention to accessories. I'll discuss wardrobe and accessories further in Chapter 5.

Approach a Feeler. Feelers have a way of sending out mixed signals. If a feeler likes you, he'll listen to your anecdotes and even share some stories of his own. Then, just when you think you've persuaded him to sign on the dotted line, he'll tactfully turn the corner and walk away. Better to slow down your pursuit of your own agenda. Greet him with a big smile and a warm handshake, and leave your structured clothing at home. You won't be judged by your appearance, but tucking a small, colorful handkerchief in your jacket pocket or tossing a shawl over one shoulder will help you make an impact on his emotions.

Approach a Judge. Dealing with a judge is simple: make a commitment and live up to it. Set goals and use benchmarks to measure your performance by objective standards. Fail to meet a judge's expectations and you'll travel a rocky road.

If you're a judge who is managing a perceiver, you may find that your perceiver employee frustrates the devil out of you with his lackadaisical concern about deadlines. When I work with P's, I deceive them by assigning earlier dates so they end up meeting my true deadline.

Approach a Perceiver. You can always try to control a perceiver by making your expectations clear, but it may be better to try to be a bit more easygoing yourself, so you won't be too disappointed when he lets you down. After all, perceivers are so easy to be around and never make anyone feel out of line—it's a trait worth rewarding with a little patience. Pressure tactics just don't work with perceivers. But if *you're* the P, recognize that not everyone is as flexible as you are. Put others at ease by assuring them that you can be depended upon, and then deliver on your promises.

YOUR DNA IN ACTION

Are You an Eagle?

Eagles, or leaders, recognize that they have the ability to assess information and take action. They have strong constitutions that help them withstand rejection. They are egocentric, which makes them want to persuade and serve as an example for others to follow. Leaders know themselves well enough to feel comfortable enlisting the aid of people or services that can supply qualities they themselves are lacking. Because they rely on the groups they assemble rather than on themselves alone, leaders can accomplish anything they can imagine. They delight in determining the pace or plan for a group. Leaders often possess balanced personalities— unless, that is, they have a Machiavellian streak and simply want to control people. True leaders rise to prominence whether they desire to lead or not, as did Margaret Thatcher.

Are You a Sheep?

Many sheep, or followers, were raised by parents who rigidly adhered to punishment and reward systems and who put authority figures such as teachers or priests (rabbis, ministers, etc.) on a pedestal. To a follower, disapproval feels like a form of punishment. Introverts tend to be followers; they're most comfortable when they're taking direction from a person in power. Some followers might have become leaders, but their drive was crushed by a neighborhood bully or an overbearing parent. They may never have revolted as teenagers to test their self-confidence.

Are You a Lone Wolf?

You might assume that every nonconformist or rebel is a lone-wolf independent, but that's not so. A rebel is simply someone who tries to make people uncomfortable or who takes pleasure in being the thorn in another person's side. A true independent is someone who has reached the point in his psyche where he achieves goals without making compromises along the way. Intuitors are generally independents. They won't discipline themselves to be led or to take the responsibility of leading. They want to answer only to themselves. They don't function well in business unless they're the top banana, in which case, they can't be truly independent because they have to assume the interests of a leader. They'd do better to be left alone in a room generating brilliant ideas.

The social world is another story. Independents can be fun to have around; they have that don't-give-a-damn attitude other people envy. If they get bored at a party, they leave. It doesn't make them feel self-conscious to walk away from something once it ceases to stimulate them because they have a certain internal strength, often coupled with other factors such as independent wealth, eccentricity, or genius. You can't sway an independent with peer pressure, threats, or bribes because lone wolves are guided by a set of immutable standards and values. There's a little streak of the independent in all of us—at some point every kid shakes off Mom and insists on doing a task by himself.

None of the three types described above is really better than the others, although most people don't like to think of themselves as sheep. But just for a moment, let's say you are a follower, and that you judge yourself harshly for fitting that description. Wouldn't it be nice to either stop judging yourself and accept the role you've chosen, or work to take on another role? Wouldn't it be nice to find a better person to hitch your star to, and focus the rest of your energy on more worthy pursuits?

If you're not comfortable with where you fit, use what you know about the components of your personality to strengthen the traits that will allow you to sit back and follow in peace, stand up and lead, or chuck the whole business and strike out alone as an independent. Then you can use your knowledge of personality types to finesse the people you socialize with. As a leader, you might assess the people you are interested in to earn their respect and make them want to join your circle. As a follower, you might try to charm someone whose parties or private clubs you want to join. As an independent, you can revel in your indifference to the whole social two-step.

THREE-SECOND OVERVIEW

Pinpointing your personality traits has given you an insight into your point of view. You've also learned how to discern the personality traits of others so you can accommodate their communicating style.

In the next chapter, you'll encounter caste systems; the levels of power within each caste; and the effect these caste systems have on your opportunity for upward mobility.

4

Where Are You, Where Are You Going?

LEVELS OF INFLUENCE

There *is* a caste system, both in the United States and around the globe. It's part of being a member of the animal kingdom. Virtually all beings, from ants to gorillas, organize themselves into a hierarchy of leaders and followers, workers and drones. Our caste system isn't officially defined the way it is in India, where there are Brahmins at the top of society and Untouchables at the bottom. Or England, where there is a vast gap between the royal family and the working class. For this reason, many Americans like to pretend class doesn't exist—but pretending won't make it go away. It may make you uncomfortable for me to talk about class because you'd rather not think about it, but if I didn't discuss it I'd be doing you a disservice. It's more constructive to recognize class systems and address them. You may not consider socioeconomic class an important issue in your life, but it comes up every time you meet new people. As they appraise your clothing, demeanor, manners, and grooming, and decide whether you're worth their time, one of their first questions is: Is this person from my own status level?

This discussion always makes me nervous, because I'm afraid that my intentions will be misconstrued. Class is a touchy subject, so let's move our focus away from it. The question of where you are and where you want to go concerns your perspective and ambition. Status levels, unlike strict definitions of the dread "C word," are determined by attitudes, values, and behavior—not necessarily determined at birth.

Nowadays status is most often determined by a person's style—the level and depth of experience, and the choices he makes based on that experience. Someone who is from a sophisticated background, who is well traveled and has been exposed to many cultures and customs, might choose to wear understated, quality clothing and behave in an especially gracious manner. That's because the hours he has spent at formal gatherings or cultural events have refined his manners and shaped his values. If you were to meet someone like this, you'd notice his savoir faire and sense of entitlement and assume he was to the manor born. But you might be wrong; nowhere is it written that you need a large bank account or a prep-school background to convey such an impression.

Someone whose experience is more limited might have been exposed to only one group of people—perhaps a group that prefers an informal style of interaction and dress. It might sound as though the sophisticated person is comfortable in more formal settings and the less sophisticated one in casual settings but, in fact, a worldly person is comfortable in almost any setting. More than that, he can make people from varied backgrounds feel comfortable around him, which the person with limited experience would find difficult.

It's an unusual way of looking at the issue of socioeconomic status. In some countries the upper levels are considered an exclusive and narrow domain. As you go up, it's assumed you will shun people who are "below" you and leave skidmarks as you drive over them during your ascendancy. Indeed, there are people like that at all levels of society. But if you think of status in terms of experience, going up means broadening your horizons rather than shrinking them. If you have developed a persona that limits you to a certain group, say by speaking with a strong regional accent or wearing grungy clothes and a wild hairstyle, your access is limited to your peers and to people in less prestigious groups. If you speak eloquently, dress well, and back it up with the social skills to put others at ease, virtually no group will exclude you.

Many clients tell me of their hunger to reach this measure of acceptance; almost all of us harbor some desire to see every door open to us. It requires training, self-discipline, and an understanding of socioeconomic structures. You must be realistic about your status on the pyramid before you're able to achieve the level of influence you desire. Begin by scanning the pyramid to locate the level where you stand, then consider any modifications you may have to make.

Level of Influence

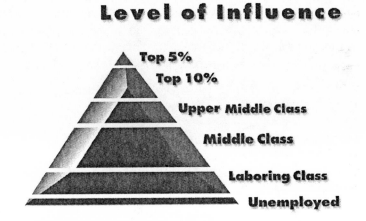

Top 5%

Top 10%

Upper Middle Class

Middle Class

Laboring Class

Unemployed

The top 5% includes a rarefied group of people who have achieved exceptional power through inheritance, business cartels, or political dominance. Mavericks have made it into this group, including Bill Gates of Microsoft, whose ingenuity fuels the current technology revolution.

The top 10% includes ambitious climbers who are exposed to a taste of the good life at association gatherings. These are the dedicated staffers who are motivated to contribute their efforts through traditional ascension in corporate life, civil service, or religious hierarchies. Needless to say, their political skills have been honed to perfection.

The largest segment in most societies is the middle class. Those in the upper levels are ambitious, striving to achieve a more comfortable lifestyle for themselves and their families. At the lower levels, those less educated survive with a limited sense of their potential.

This pyramid may reflect the way things happen for a small sector at the top, but it doesn't illustrate the access they have to other people or to opportunities in the business and social world. It may not be fair, but it's real.

True, to a great degree status is determined at birth. Within moments of entering the world, it's clear that a Rockefeller baby, for instance, will have more opportunities than a baby born to an average family struggling to make ends meet. But each of us can learn how to free ourselves from the constraints of our inherited culture and move beyond it to open doors in both our careers and social lives. How? By answering these three questions:

1. What does my persona tell others about my standing?
2. Am I content to be labeled a member of that group?
3. If not, which group do I aspire to join?

BUILD A POWER BASE: POWER SECRET #4

If attitudes and behavior are what determine which socioeconomic group others will assume you belong to, how do you determine where you are and where you want to go? I've developed a guide to the identifying characteristics that typically apply to each of six societal levels. This list may get your back up, and I don't blame you; at first it might seem rigidly stereotypical. Still, it has proven to be an accurate classification system that will help you not only to see yourself but to make quick assessments of others based on very little information. Such a system is especially helpful when you're trying to decide how to approach an interviewer or manager who comes from a background that's different from yours.

As you look at the list, notice that each group has been given a number from 1 to 6, loosely corresponding to the prestige accorded it by society. The list also roughly follows the economic pyramid on p. 69, but the groups are less defined by dollars and birth than by conduct and values.

To find the unifying characteristics of Group 3/Strivers, for example, look for all the attributes numbered "3." You will then come up with a detailed profile of someone who is likely to be:

- A striver with a sense of potential status
- An extrovert who seeks acceptance
- A cost-conscious manager who interprets policy
- A political opportunist who seeks support
- A traditional person who is stable and conventional
- Someone with goody-two-shoes manners who is too constrained
- A member of professional associations and civic groups
- A patron of quality restaurants who attends small dinner parties
- A business-class traveler who leases or owns an American car
- A consumer of purchases at better department and specialty stores
- A vacationer who prefers group tours and time-shares
- A sports enthusiast who prefers power boating, golf, and skiing

The following case study is an example of someone who managed to jump past two social levels, moving from group "4" to level "1" through maverick behavior and plenty of nerve.

Case Study: Robert, Age 55

An ambitious fast-track advertising executive, Robert had already gone far beyond his roots by the time he retained me to help him move confidently into more sophisticated circles. He desperately wanted to overcome the limitations of his middle-class background to rise above the conservative lifestyle provided by his father and mother. When his small company was acquired by a larger firm, he knew he lacked the social graces to be accepted in the new culture. Earlier successes had come about through a combination of drive and charisma, not savoir faire.

Everything about him smacked of a small-town upbringing, including his polyester suits acquired at discount outlets. Robert looked totally out of place in New York advertising circles—a diamond in the rough who needed polishing. To begin his transformation, we spent Saturdays refurbishing his wardrobe with custom-tailored Brioni suits, Sea Island cotton shirts by Charvet, Hermès ties, and Ferragamo shoes. (I'll explain in detail how to choose appropriate clothing and other surface status symbols in the next chapter.) Unfortunately, his comfort level was so challenged by the status change that he later admitted his new clothes were sitting in his closet, unworn! Robert was too insecure to venture far from his office to face a more refined audience. He needed a total make-over—from inside out—Pygmalion in reverse.

He had to be taught the manners and protocol required at lofty levels, including how to eat Continental style. He also needed a better haircut, so I took him to a well-known stylist who shaped and colored his gray hair. Before long, looking debonair and feeling more self-assured, Robert began going to cultural events, gallery openings, and charity affairs, all the while honing his new social skills.

Although Robert wasn't prepared to pursue memberships in exclusive clubs in a major city, he did gain admission to a country club in a Midwest community where he often traveled on business. This atmosphere served as a comfortable testing ground for the game he wanted to play in better circles, and it was an ideal place to check out his new style on a higher class of people.

As a former salesman who knew how to impress people with invitations to promotional activities, he got on the board members' good side by using his business perks to take some of them to the Olympics and other major sporting events. He knew this was one way to leap over social barriers—and he was right. People at every level are vulnerable to a good time even when the invitation comes from a social maverick.

Robert's drive paid off when he became chairman of a conglomerate—seven years after we began working on his image.

This story illustrates an important point about social strata and conformity; if you want to enter an exclusive group, you've got to change your behavior to match that of its members or have some unusual appeal that attracts them. It takes a great deal of discipline and self-awareness to achieve social and professional goals. Not everyone has to try to move up. But if you want to break out of your current situation, you must understand and accept the mores of different social groups for what they are. And if you decide you want to enter one, it's easier if you adjust your bearing accordingly.

People make the trip a lot tougher when they try to distinguish themselves as mavericks. The only thing that can protect you when you're an aberration is your influence. That can mean money, connections, or a commodity people want. Without such influence, you'll find the reception is cool.

My interest is not in reinforcing or praising the rigid behavior that's necessary to gain entrée to a certain social or business milieu, but if you can accept the strict standards that exist and adopt them in order to pass the warriors at the gate, you may end up with more freedom on the other side.

After all, you won't get the chance to perform if you can't get inside the door. Think of the extent to which medical residents, corporate finance analysts, and young lawyers get beaten up early in their careers. The system threatens to sap their strength and vitality until they learn how to prioritize and take shortcuts. As they are given more responsibility and perform well, they are accepted into the inner circle. Oddly, it is this acceptance of responsibility and this ability to prove themselves that gives them their freedom: the freedom that comes with being admitted to an elite group and being valued by powerful people.

Most of us begin life as diamonds in the rough. As we go up against the grinding wheel of life, we become more polished and attractive. We also learn that some people are incapable of appreciating our clarity, cut, and color. Or, if they do recognize our worth, they try to hold us back. In either case, we have to move on to a place where people have the capacity to value our brilliance.

To detect how others evaluate you within three seconds, read on.

POWER PROFILES

Personal Status

1. Eagle	sense of entitlement
2. Originator	sense of nonconformity
3. Striver	sense of potential status
4. Survivor	sense of swimming upstream

5. Confederate	sense of brotherhood
6. Impoverished	sense of inequality

Personal Confidence

1. Egocentric	subjective
2. Altruistic	selfless
3. Extrovert	seeks acceptance
4. Acquiescent	seeks acceptance
5. Compliant	seeks acceptance
6. Unconventional	defies acceptance

Professional Orientation

1. Policy setter	long-term conceptualizer
2. Visionary	innovator, product developer, spender
3. Manager	interprets policy, proactive
4. Producer	assignment-oriented, time-conscious
5. Maintainer	technician, repair person, time-conscious
6. Nonproducer	unemployed, semimotivated

Fortune-Hunting Orientation

1. Adventuresome	shrewd competitor
2. High risk-taker	resourceful
3. Sensible	political opportunist
4. Guarded	conservative
5. Dedicated follower	collective bargainer
6. Moocher	subsidy seeker

Personal Style

1. Urbane	diplomatic, sophisticated
2. Eccentric	nonconformist, open-minded
3. Traditional	stable, conventional
4. Conservative	restrained, narrow
5. Conscientious	cautious, prudent
6. Drifter	unpolished, narrow-minded

Education

1. Graduate degree, foreign study, preparatory schools
2. Special degree or training

3. Undergraduate degree
4. Junior college degree
5. High school or trade school degree
6. Partial schooling or dropout

Social Amenities
1. Formal, gracious, articulate, deferential
2. Less formal, ever ready to assist in solving problems
3. Goody-two-shoes manners, less discerning
4. Uptight, uneasy, less gracious, judgmental
5. Shy, reserved, cautious, kindly
6. Brash, colorful language, street smart

Alliances
1. Exclusive club memberships
2. Aesthetic, creative associations
3. Association and group memberships
4. YMCA, YWCA, health clubs
5. Religious affiliations, lodges, volunteer organizations
6. Neighborhood activities

Dining
1. Gourmet restaurants, private clubs, formal dinner parties
2. Ethnic restaurants, health food, home cooking
3. Quality restaurants, small dinner parties
4. Family restaurants, potluck suppers
5. Family style, home cooking
6. Fast food

Transportation
1. Prestige cars, Land Rover, limousine, Learjet, Concorde
2. Sports car, convertible, old Volkswagen
3. Chrysler, Buick, business-class travel
4. Station wagon, camper, secondhand car, coach-class travel
5. Public transportation, economy-class travel
6. Secondhand van, truck, bicycle

Apparel
1. Custom-tailored wardrobe, designer clothes and accessories
2. Original, ethnic, colorful separates and comfortable shoes
3. Better department and specialty store ready-to-wear
4. Discount store and sale merchandise

    5. Casual wear, homemade separates

    6. Jeans, T-shirts, easy-care apparel

Recreation

    1. Exclusive resorts, clubs, weekend homes, exotic vacations

    2. Retreats, artists' colonies, museums, concerts

    3. Group travel tours, time-sharing condominiums

    4. Amusement parks, camping

    5. Church parties, bingo, zoos

    6. Public park games, television

Sports

    1. Sailing, flying, polo, tennis, golf, skiing

    2. Bridge, backgammon, chess, puzzles

    3. Power-boating, golf, skiing

    4. Bicycling, fishing, swimming, hiking

    5. Spectator and team sports

    6. Sandlot sports

Did you find that most of your defining traits and preferences belong to a particular group? Few people will identify with every attribute in a given category right down the line, but most of us find that the great majority of our predilections fit with one of the levels described above. You can see how easy it is to use this list of traits to compose a profile of someone you barely know or haven't even met. Ask around about the person's lifestyle. All you need to hear is that he's a member of an exclusive golf club who drives a Ferrari, has an MBA or Ph.D., and wears custom-tailored suits, and most likely you're dealing with a Level 1 powerhouse. Later in this chapter, I'll give you tips about how to tailor your impression to suit people at different levels.

If you're still having trouble figuring out where you fit on this socioeconomic scale, take a test I call "Social Comfort Zone." I ask my client to think of an item that costs about the same price no matter where you buy it. For women, it might be cosmetics; for men, perhaps ties. I'd ask the woman which brand she chooses—a drugstore line or one that can be found only in department stores? If it's the latter, at which department store does she choose to buy the item? Is there a more or less exclusive retailer in as convenient a location she could patronize? If so, why doesn't she?

Sometimes I'll discover that the woman works at an office three blocks from a swank department store, but she drives to a mall on the weekends to buy her cosmetics at a less glittery chain instead. Why? We all like convenience, but it may be that she doesn't feel comfortable shopping in the exclusive store. This information can tell her a good deal about where she fits on the social comfort zone scale.

Now examine your fantasies. If you could shop (or take a vacation, to use another social comfort zone question) anywhere, where would you go? Your answer should tell you something about your aspirations. It also indicates how you like to be treated. When the woman selects a store in which to buy her cosmetics, she is indicating that she is comfortable with the level of graciousness and deference that will be shown to her by the store's employees.

Again, acknowledging that there are subtly defined status levels in our society can make people uneasy. Regardless, it's helpful to know your current level, and to determine whether there is something pushing you to feel discontent with your position. Whatever you decide, remember that my program isn't about climbing, it's about security and insecurity. Are you secure enough to move around many of society's social levels? Even if you're happy with where you are, you will need to be compatible with clients and bosses on several levels in order to maximize your potential. Once you've determined the degree to which change is your goal, you're ready to work on the package you present to the world and the impression you make.

Unlike some of the other changes I help clients to make, moving up one or two levels on the status scale requires a long-term commitment—perhaps two or three years per level. I'm not a psychologist, but I've observed in my practice that the psyche can't handle radical modifications in values and behavior any faster. I've also found that it's nearly impossible to make a Horatio Alger-type leap over more than two levels—period—for the same reason. It's too much of a shock to the system. When I named my quick test "Social Comfort Zone," I did it for a reason; the measure of comfort you feel with any group of people usually dictates your social zone. It's their standard of behavior, not their financial resources, that should attract you. A perfect example is the comedienne Roseanne, who once said that she was everyone's worst nightmare: "white trash with money." Her observation is interesting because, no matter how financially successful she has become, she deliberately hasn't changed her behavior to conform to affluent society. She probably isn't comfortable in a disciplined environment, so she chooses to be a misfit who doesn't have to worry about paying the bills.

THE MATURITY SPIRAL

My theory on maturity is that life isn't a vertical climb, or a circle of events that keep coming around. It's a spiral that wends its way to personal enlightenment. It's not uncommon to encounter a challenging situation that is similar to one you've experienced before. If you've "been there, done that," you know how to handle current situations—without repeating past mistakes—by modifying your behavior. You also recognize when it's wiser to avoid being egocentric by accommodating another person's need ahead of your own. The secret to success is knowing which choice to make.

Advancing within the social ranks requires more than discipline, self-knowledge, and drive. It requires maturity. The kind you gain from expressing yourself along the way. As a baby you cried for help, as a toddler you expressed your independence: "I can do it myself." But this newfound self-reliance reverts to another form of compliance at school, when you learn what it means to obey a teacher who sets the rules of behavior. As a student, you are not allowed to roam independently—you must learn to conform to succeed. As a teenager you hit another stage of independence when the desire to please your peers outweighs the need to please your parents; you might experiment with extremes in behavior, appearance, and language. But the day comes when either college or a job beckons, and once again you must meet someone else's standards.

Eventually, as an adult, you leave home to build your own life and assemble your own circle of friends, but still there is someone—whether a wife or husband at home or a manager at work—to whom you must show at least some deference.

During this tug-of-war between independence and conformity, each stage in your development is a vital link to maturity. If you miss or skip a stage, something in your nature drives you back to complete that development. For example, if you never rebelled or broke some rules as an adolescent, you will probably lack a certain adventuresome spirit as an adult. You may internalize your resentment of the people or the forces that caused you to curb your urge to disobey and begin to blame yourself entirely. After a time, you may transfer those feelings of anger and frustration to your wife, lover, or boss. The skipped stage becomes as irritating as a mosquito bite, impossible to soothe.

People who have allowed themselves the opportunity to go against the tide—not doing anything immoral or dangerous, simply something naughty—discover they won't burn in hell. The bottom line is that completing each stage of life, especially the nonconformist ones, teaches everyone not to be so hard on themselves. Personal tolerance helps you become tolerant of others and allows for missteps as well. Such an attitude preserves the unique, risk-taking spirit you had at birth.

I've noticed that people I've worked with who ascend to the top of the maturity spiral are those who are less threatened by the prospect of moving beyond their social stratum. These mature individuals function at full capacity, utilizing whatever talent they've been given with enough self-assurance to break through imaginary glass ceilings.

Those who never leave their rebellious stage are handicapped by a lack of self-discipline, and they have trouble fulfilling their commitments: their social behavior flouts society's rules, making it difficult for them to recognize the codes of the system they have to navigate. The ones who conform too much, by contrast, can become the Caspar Milquetoasts, who sit at a desk and "yes" people to death. Both types are stuck at an immature level of development; neither is free to take risks.

POWER STRATA

By now you've probably come to a decision about whether you'd like to move up a socioeconomic level. But even if you're happy where you are, you can benefit from learning how to finesse the members of other groups. Moreover, your work may involve marketing to different social levels, and you will need to know how such people think in order to sell to them.

Top 5% or "Eagles"

Heritage and bloodlines mean more than performance here—even more than money. In fact, it's often true that the members of this group have less money than the so-called *nouveau riche,* who may occupy the level below.

It takes two or three generations to launch a family into this elite orbit, just as it took two or three generations for the original American business barons to clean up their image through philanthropy and community projects before emerging as members of the old money crowd. Once there, members of this group tend to sequester themselves, removing their children from public life by sending them off to boarding schools. They are considerate and civil to the people of lower strata who make their lives run smoothly, from the valet to the doorman, but they are more likely to treat them in an autocratic fashion than to view them as equals. A lot of eccentric odd ducks exist in this circle, and no wonder—financial independence has a way of exempting people from the rules by which the rest of us live.

As you might imagine, interacting with these people requires you to draw on your most refined manners and show deference. If you have anything in your wardrobe that can stand up to their classic, often custom-made attire, by all means wear it. Be self-effacing and unassuming; refrain from asking direct personal questions (see "Artful Conversation" in the next chapter) and project an aura of confidence, even if you are secretly feeling in over your head. This is when you become a good listener!

Top 10% or Entrepreneur and Nonconformist

This group is open to all newcomers with a key to the door: gain entrance to so-called polite society through major philanthropic gifts, high political office, or business acumen. As high up as its members seem to be, there is a genuine striver element here; many new money *arrivistes* are ever conscious of solidifying their position in order to pass down the legacy to their children. Except, perhaps, for its newer members, this group and the top group are equal in terms of their old-fashioned ideas about status, although they express them differently. The entrepreneurial group might opt for a less restrictive environment in favor of one that is more intellectually or creatively stimulating.

Although this group is more open than the one above it, that's not saying very much. Like the eagles, entrepreneurs are rare and seldom interface publicly on a business basis. They consummate deals in private clubs, on yachts, or in their homes. What forces them to pay attention to outsiders is some quality or talent that qualifies the newcomer for membership. Among these qualities are physical beauty, athletic prowess, performing talent, superior intelligence, definitive bloodlines, landownership, or creative genius. It is in this way that actors, models, writers, and enterprising executives sometimes manage to break in.

One point worth making is that, though people might assume that the social elite discriminate against them, less privileged people are often equally guilty of reverse discrimination, preemptively rejecting those they perceive to be more advantaged. It's better to keep an open mind. First, you can't be sure whether someone *is* from an exceptionally privileged background, and second, even if you're right, it's not their fault they were born into a life of ease. Moreover, their affluence hasn't guaranteed them a breezy time—difficult personal circumstances are often part of the package. Accept them and accept yourself during your encounters, and both parties will benefit from the exchange.

Upper Middle Class or Striver

The country club crowd is a group whose members are well traveled and who send their children to dancing class, possibly prep school, and to superior private colleges. Although there is a real keep-up-with-the-Joneses element here, members of this crowd are not nearly as competitive as they might be. In fact, they are quick to open their doors and hearts to those whose lifestyle and beliefs are in line with their own. Rather than trying to climb over others to get ahead, they seek to enlarge their circle and make things easier for others. There are a lot of mentors on this level, people who find joy in empowering others who meet their standards or values. One reason is that many members of the upper middle class have made the jump from middle class by pursuing a lucrative professional career, and they take great pride in their status and the power that goes with it.

By the same token, adults in this group help their children remain within its ranks as they grow up. Clubs offer junior memberships so that young people can afford luxurious amenities. Because of the strong family bond, parents consider the favors they give their children a privilege rather than a sacrifice.

The ethic of giving extends beyond family circles, making the upper middle class in many ways the foundation of society. These are the people who support community efforts and charitable groups. Taking pride in making the world a better place, strivers abide by the law, vote, and contribute, contribute, contribute. If you want to become one of them, you must adopt this benevolent spirit. On a more practical level, behavior is what most often disqualifies wannabes from membership, so mind your manners—particularly at the table. See that you live up to their standards of manners and magnanimity and you may well be taken on by a mentor, who will help you gain entree to their ranks.

Middle Class or Survivor

There's an interesting misperception about the middle class that I'd like to correct. I've heard people say that they are nervous about trying to go to a higher social level because they'll have to become more constrained. That's partly true; as I've said, you must refine your behavior as you ascend the social ladder. But the middle class is the most restrictive, most exclusionary group there is. If this seems counterintuitive, think about someone like Elizabeth Taylor. As a wealthy celebrity, she can get away with marrying eight times. So can someone on the lowest rung of society, who is free to marry over and over, or even give birth to children without benefit of marriage, and not be shunned by her peers. But in the middle class—what a scandal!

Why is it this way? Because at either end of the social spectrum there's virtually no movement. It's almost impossible to be dislodged from your station, and this sense of entitlement at the top or hopelessness at the bottom breeds liberal behavior. Fashion trends, for instance, start at the very top or the very bottom of society, where people aren't likely to be ostracized by their peers and don't depend on their appearance for acceptance.

"Safe" is the watchword of the middle class. Conservative and conformist, the masses lack the self-assurance to move up and thus take pains to rein in those who do. Ambition is considered a threat. This is the boss who is intimidated when a young newcomer thinks like an executive; the manager who squashes the upstart's innovative ideas. It happens in the social world too; members of the middle class join fraternal-type clubs that tightly define their interests or backgrounds and force members to work their way up through endless committees before they're in decision-making circles. Even once they've made it, the clan mentality often dictates that someone in the club member's family had to pave the way for others to be considered acceptable.

This behavior stems from the Calvinistic attitude that says each of us must walk the same twenty miles in the snow. The middle class has a hazing mentality; it values rites of passage, never allowing anyone to skip a single bureaucratic step. Indeed, a good number of people at this stratum work at low- to mid-level government jobs. If any level of society is paranoid about exclusionary status, it's this one, because those within these boundaries are aware of the constant danger of falling off the ladder or getting knocked off by someone on the way up.

To work successfully with this group, you've got to make them feel secure and important by sharing your ideas and occasionally allowing others to take credit for your activities. To become one of them, you must build their faith in you and help them to see the advantage in supporting you. Still, it's extremely difficult to meet this challenge without connections or a mentor. It might be better to recognize the limitations of succeeding and acknowledge that it's just a short step from this level to where you may really want to go: the upper middle class. Here's how Matt made the leap.

Case Study: Matt, 44

Matt worked in banquet sales for a hotel chain. Charming, capable, and attractive, he and his wife Debbie and their two children lived in the same middle- to lower-middle-class residential community where Matt grew up. When he wasn't at work, Matt hung around with his old friends from grammar school, none of whom had achieved nearly his level of success.

Matt told me that he had built a productive team of associates around the country who were surpassing their sales targets, yet he couldn't convince management to move him into a top sales job. It was easy to see why—he hadn't changed his appearance as he climbed up the company ladder. The first time we met, he wore a polyester suit with a psychedelic multicolored tie. He surely fit in with his chums in the old neighborhood, but he was an outsider among his peers at work. At the same time, I sensed in Matt a desire to change and couldn't figure out why he hadn't done so.

I soon discovered the answer. Matt and Debbie had grown up together, and she was especially wedded to the past. Like Matt, she dressed below their means, and collected bargains purchased at the local mall. I explained that it was important to maintain relationships with childhood friends, but that we all had to understand that when our circumstances change, old friends can't always keep up. It's possible to remain loyal and yet move ahead to new horizons, new friendships, new experiences.

At first, Debbie was concerned about what her friends would say if she and Matt bought a foreign car, vacationed abroad, or allowed themselves the other luxuries they'd dreamed of but hadn't acted on. I asked Debbie why her fear of being rejected by their neighbors and friends should inhibit her dreams. Just asking that question made Debbie realize they'd outgrown their neighborhood. After working through my program, Matt and Debbie decided to sell their house and move to a more affluent neighborhood with a more diverse population. They still saw their old friends although, as I'd warned, some were threatened by Matt and Debbie's success and ended the friendship. But the family also began to meet people who were more broad-minded, and they discovered that they fit in nicely.

Matt's career took off like a shot. He was promoted several times and became vice president of the hotel chain. His family joins him on his travels to meetings around the world, where they receive quite an education in protocol.

Laboring Class, Semiskilled Worker, and Below

Obviously, many more people at this level are seeking to rise above it than are striving to reach it. Forever swimming upstream, the laboring-class or semiskilled worker feels on the edge of society and seeks acceptance for his contributions. At the same time, he feels a tremendous loyalty to his roots and the philosophy of his family and resists changing his packaging in order to better his position. There's a defensiveness about befriending people outside the circle, as if forging relationships with other groups would be a betrayal of one's heritage.

Interestingly, this group has a great deal in common with the upper middle class, who contribute hours of their free time to charitable organizations. These are the volunteer firefighters, the housewives who volunteer at homeless shelters and found groups like MADD (Mothers Against Drunk Driving). If there's a fight on the subway, they'll jump out of their seats and intervene. Samaritans are nice people who fix their own appliances and pay union dues. Lacking in money, connections, or social expertise, they make things happen through their hard work and sheer numbers rather than through influence. Breaking away and moving up would mean abandoning their roots, which is more than their pride will usually allow—even if they wish that were not the case.

Throughout this chapter I've tied work status to social status; here's a client history that demonstrates further why they can't be separated.

Case History: Jane, 45

A few years ago, Jane came to me for help in honing her political skills to get her out of an undesirable job track; what she didn't realize was that she needed to increase her social status to show her superiors that she was sophisticated enough to switch to the job track she preferred. Jane had started out as an accessories sales manager at one of the now defunct Bonwit Teller department stores. Once she moved into buying, she immediately produced a record-breaking profit and hoped that she might be transferred into corporate buying, but the store insisted she stay in the local branch and learn administrative and management skills by becoming a store manager.

I wasn't surprised that Bonwit's corporate headquarters didn't want Jane; she wasn't their "type." Most Bonwit's customers were members of the upper middle class, whereas Jane's image was decidedly middle class. She spoke rapidly with a grating Midwestern twang and came across as a human lap dog—eager to please, overly candid and casual, lacking reserve. Most off-putting was her personal packaging; there was too much of everything. Big hair, high-heeled shoes, oversized dangling earrings, dark lip pencil painted around the edge of a pink mouth. Her appearance was more detrimental than it would be to most people because, as a fashion buyer, she needed to look like a forecaster, a trendsetter.

I realized that I needed to open her eyes about social status and the ways it could limit progress in the business world. We lunched at an elegant restaurant and, as we ate, I asked her to people-watch with me. Looking around the room, Jane identified diners who would fit in at corporate headquarters versus those who appeared likely to top out on the local level. The conversation turned to the movie *Working Girl* and its lessons about how people do a quick read on others and then use any subsequent information to back up their initial impression. No matter how worthwhile the secretary's ideas were, no one at the company would give her the time of day until she boosted her look and demeanor to that of an upper-class player. Jane was fascinated with this notion and started to think in terms of a comprehensive makeover to get the same result.

We began with her clipped, flat, monotone voice. To help Jane see that her voice lacked the lyrical, inviting qualities it needed, I asked her to call her own answering machine and listen to the tape. As a result, she went to a speech improvement coach and began to view her voice as an instrument of persuasion rather than a tool to relay information.

Jane lacked the body discipline exhibited by well-mannered people; she gesticulated to excess, had poor table manners, and crossed her legs improperly (believe it or not, even *this* is important, and I'll explain the correct method for crossing your legs in the next chapter). She learned these skills, refurbished her wardrobe, and had her hair restyled. Now it was time to bring Jane into the world she wanted to join. Acting as her mentor, I exposed her to clubs where she took lessons in tennis, golf, and sailing, all the while scrutinizing the behavior of the club's members. Jane then pampered herself with a weekend at a luxurious spa and a wine tour through California's Napa Valley—environments in which she made new contacts in her desired social group.

When Jane returned from her trip, I was stunned. Poised, dignified, and confident, she had gained the bearing of someone who had grown up with the country club crowd. Jane was wearing a blue designer suit and a beautiful starfish pin covered with diamonds and rubies, which she carried off with panache (only she knew for sure whether the stones were real!). It was time to pursue her agenda at Bonwit's.

"You're not a security guard," I told Jane. "You're not going to open the store in the morning and lock it up at night." Taking an enormous gamble, Jane rejected the company's offer to make her a store manager, risking her mentor's wrath. Instead she spent the next few months building relationships with people in corporate headquarters whose positions were a level or two above hers. Whenever she had time, she'd call important contacts at headquarters and ask them for trend information. It wasn't long before people knew who she was. These contacts got her an interview for the position of merchandising administrator of a special fashion program. Jane got the job and within a year doubled her volume and was given greater responsibilities.

As Jane enlarged her social circle, she experienced some resistance from her family and old friends, who considered her growth a sign of disloyalty. I explained that her middle-class family's reaction was quite common, and suggested that she might try to explain that she was broadening her power base rather than leaving her friends and family behind.

THE BUSINESS CASTE SYSTEM

Jane discovered that there's a caste system in the business world that is as firmly entrenched as the one in the social world. Moreover, the two are intertwined. If Jane wanted to rise within her company, she had to polish her social profile. She had to appear not only capable of handling the work but also equal to the protocol involved in dealing with people at that level. Her managers weren't necessarily wrong in holding that view; the higher you rise in a company, the more important it is to understand diplomacy. Here's why.

Each level in business has its own unique profile, as you will see on the following chart. Read it to consider which level of power is best suited for your talents.

*SENIOR MANAGEMENT: those who have risen above and beyond
the bureaucracy*

Dynamic	Bottom-line-oriented
Charismatic	Status-conscious
Risk-taker	Competitive
Visionary	Possessive
Egocentric and shrewd	Singular in purpose

*MIDDLE MANAGEMENT: those who work within the existing bu-
reaucracy and are useful in achieving production goals and getting
people to work together*

Interpret policy	Set standards
Evaluate performances	Motivate subordinates
Barter-oriented	Political

*STAFF: cautious workers who require defined roles and expecta-
tions*

Technically skilled	Task-oriented
Inflexible	Frustrated by change
Time-conscious	Street smart
Loyal followers	Opportunistic

Notice how many of the traits that define employees at different
levels within a company correspond to the characteristics of the
societal levels discussed earlier in this chapter. The economic and
work pyramids align as well; the most sophisticated senior managers earn many times the pay of staff. If you want to rise within the
corporate caste system, you must rise within the social caste system—or convince your superiors that you possess the social skills
practiced by those at the upper levels.

Behavior at the highest levels of the business hierarchy is different because the goals are different. Staff members are just trying to
get their jobs done. A manager gives them a task and a timetable in
which to finish it, and the staff members crank out the product. No
diplomacy necessary there. The manager, however, has to keep his
subordinates' morale high enough for them to be productive and
meet his objectives. That requires some diplomacy.

The leader of the company is in an entirely different league. His success or failure rests almost exclusively on his ability to deal with a wide variety of people. Union leaders must feel he's made concessions to their workers. Competitors who become stragetic partners must feel he will help them make money rather than use the alliance to steal their ideas or customers. Suppliers must feel they're getting a fair price for their goods. And on and on. At the top of a corporation, negotiation is the primary activity. People at the low end of the social spectrum seldom ascend to this level in business because their limited experience has not prepared them to use the subtle psychological tactics involved.

Do you have the social expertise to go where you want to go in business? To determine where new clients fit within their companies' culture, I ask them to describe what they do and what effect the job has on their workplace.

Senior Management

When clients talk to me about the big picture, especially if they've taken a moment to recognize my intellectual need to be made a partner in the conversation, I know they're ready for the big time. These clients explain how competitive their company's product or service may be, demonstrating that they understand its status in the marketplace. As our conversation continues, they continually draw me into the dialogue, never allowing the topic to become the focus of our interaction. If they want something from me, they put themselves in a secondary role, making me buy into the concept so that the idea seems a collaboration rather than a request. Timing is important to the senior manager, who is adept at putting his ego aside to give others a feeling of ownership of the manager's ideas, all the better to achieve his goal later. Using these nonthreatening techniques of persuasion is what helps leaders to build a grass roots constituency of people who will endorse them both in and out of their presence.

Middle Management

When clients talk to me about politics, about whom they know, it tells me they've matured to the stage where they're learning the value of charm. They understand you can't manipulate someone and achieve your goal without savoir faire or some sort of finesse. They might emphasize their managerial skills or describe a difficult personnel situation they were able to solve. Middle management is interested in trade-offs—exchanging favors for a bigger slice of the budget, for example. Some managers have the potential to think beyond their sphere and move up to a leadership role, whereas others become so involved in bartering that they lose their flexibility and stop the clock on their careers.

Staff

When clients talk to me about their technical skills, I know they're stuck at the bottom—I hope temporarily. That's because they don't realize that skill is just the beginning; marketing the skill is what will allow them to effect change rather than serve someone else's agenda. The lower he is on the company totem pole, the more likely a staffer is to express a lack of flexibility—to complain about changes that have negatively impacted his division.

Just as there are three status levels within each company, there are three levels of customers. Marketing specialists know where to reach each level: the elite market, the popular market, and the mass market. If we decided to focus on a particular audience to sell them an exercise machine, we might reach the elite market through country clubs, the popular market through health clubs, and the mass market through the YMCA or YWCA. By now you know where you fit in the social and the business hierarchies. Which audience do you belong to? Do you understand the needs of the other audiences? Demonstrating an ability to appreciate their motivations will help you achieve your goals in the business world.

However you break it down, by socioeconomic level, social traits, business hierarchy, or commercial audience, you're obligated in all your interactions to market yourself. Stay where you are or move up, but remember that the other groups are out there. You encounter them in the workplace, on the street, in stores, in movie theaters. You can't escape them or isolate yourself from them. Understand them, learn to cultivate them, and you will have more freedom from social concerns than if you tried to ignore them.

I've said before that transforming yourself from within is about becoming a better person, not about social climbing. There are superior people to be found at all levels—you don't have to improve your position in life to find them.

Social climbing, in fact, is not about becoming a better person, it's about being selfish and advancing yourself at the expense of others. Instead, think of working on your social skills as a means of broadening your opportunities so you'll have a larger audience to influence for good. A bigger arena and the power to effect change for the people within it—there's a worthy goal.

THREE-SECOND OVERVIEW

Take a good look around. Whether you like it or not, you're a member of a caste system that is alive and well, with definite rules of behavior at every level. Maybe you're satisfied with your status quo, or maybe you've decided you want to move up a notch with your fine talent. In the next chapter, I'll tell you how to make a favorable impression at any level of society.

5

Polish the Package

A behavioral scientist has suggested that appearance counts for 55% of the impression we make, voice 38%, and the substance of the conversation just 7%. Considering those figures, it's foolish to overlook the importance of grooming and manners. Still, even though outward appearance is the fastest three-second impression maker and the easiest to alter, it's the thing my clients resist the most. Too dramatic a change seems to disturb their psyches.

An attractive exterior and demeanor draw a favorable response from those with the power to help you move ahead or to hold you back. Clearly it pays to improve on nature's gifts. Research indicates that the most successful people combine Old World charm with an understanding of today's cutthroat reality. Without style, ambition is merely aggressive.

Here's a list of the components that make a first impression—the one that no amount of intelligent conversation can overturn.

IMPRESSION MAKERS

- Eye contact: direct focus eye to eye
- Overall appearance: impeccable and well groomed
- Poise, bearing, posture, stride: confident

- Personal physical condition: healthy and vigorous
  - Hair: squeaky clean
  - Skin: clear, healthy, odorless
  - Fingernails: well manicured
  - Teeth: pearly white and straight
- Personal grooming: clean and stylish
  - Makeup: subtle and understated
  - Hair style: off the face and under control
  - Facial hair: clean cut, preferably beardless
- Wardrobe condition: fresh, clean, pressed
  - Polished shoes
  - Clean clothes
- Fashion statement: timeless style and high-quality material
- Accessories: understated
  - Rings, watch, cuff links: fine quality
  - Earrings, bracelet, necklace, pin: tailored and conservative
- Handshake: firm, inside web of thumb to inside web of thumb
- Seated posture:
  - Spine erect, head at right angles to the body
  - Feet parallel at all times, no more than 15 inches apart
- Hands relaxed, palms down
- Briefcase in good condition
- Business card: black or dark blue ink on white or cream card stock
- Writing instrument: designer pen
- Writing pad: white (not yellow), encased in a folder
- Conversational ability
  - Sound, pace, enunciation communicated clearly
  - Charismatic, sophisticated
  - Worldly, open, sharing, empathetic
- Intelligence, diplomacy, tact
  - Indirect inquiries, nonprobing statements
- Perceptions of entitlement
  - Self-aware, yet respectful of others
- Departure: final impression
  - Gracious

People prefer being entertained to being educated, which goes to show that stimulating a person emotionally is the first step toward communicating with him. Your clothing and manner are part of the package you use to attract attention and make a connection. Remember that in business you dress as a sign of respect for others and the position they hold, not for your own comfort or for self-expression. Take your cue from the other person and the environment, rather than strictly from your own preferences or taste. That's how you create a bond of commonality between yourself and the person you're trying to persuade.

People who are open to modifying these attributes have ego strength: so much confidence in what's underneath that they don't find it threatening to contemplate adjusting their manners or clothing to make others more comfortable. Remember the theater analogy from Chapter 1? Business and social life are the stage, and we are the actors. Costume is just a tool we use to help create the illusion. I'm not telling you to run out and blow your savings on a designer wardrobe. I'm telling you to dress the part, whatever that requires. It may even mean dressing down, as in the case study that follows.

Case Study: Connie, Age 42

Connie left a small public relations firm, where she had promoted a well-known fashion accessory, to accept a position with a large international public relations firm. In her new role she gained an impressive title and increased responsibility. At her previous workplace she and her colleagues had dressed informally, so she spent a significant sum of money on designer clothing to upgrade her wardrobe to the level of her new post. Unfortunately, she had neglected to find out that employees at her new office dressed as casually as those at her small firm. When Connie waltzed in that first day wearing a shocking pink Christian Lacroix suit, she immediately alienated a colleague who sat casually dressed in the next office. This woman, whom I'll call Ann, had pulled herself up by her bootstraps and had been with the firm for six years. She knew all the beasts in the forest and could have been helpful to a newcomer like Connie, but she perceived that Connie was trying to show her up with her fashionable clothes.

This wasn't the case at all. Connie was thinking in terms of impressing her clients with her wardrobe, and she was right to try. The mistake she made was to overlook the necessity of building rapport with her peers and getting them into her corner. Ann was powerful enough to bury Connie before she even had a chance to invite a client to lunch.

Connie needed to make a friend of this woman. The way to bond with Ann was visually, because that's obviously how Connie had offended her. Looking at Connie, it was clear to me that her designer clothes were only part of what had irritated Ann so much. When the conversation turned to the techniques for building a powerful but friendly image, Connie said, "Camille, I'm not cutting my hair." Amazingly enough, I hadn't even mentioned it.

Hair

Ann didn't like Connie because of her debutante-like appearance. The long hair and short skirt seemed to emphasize her sex appeal and indicated an attempt to use that sex appeal to wield power. The fact that Connie jumped to the conclusion that I was going to suggest she change her hairstyle reinforced my impression that she *was* using her long hair as a come-on.

In fact, shoes and hair reveal more than any other aspect of appearance about your social status. These are the two vanity points—top and bottom—that reflect your taste and what you think of yourself. Well-made shoes, in good condition, indicate a personal concern for comfort. (I'll talk more about shoes later in this chapter.) When you respect other people, you maintain a professional image by keeping your hair well groomed and appropriately styled. For both men and women, hair sends a message about whether you're trying to draw unnecessary attention from the opposite sex.

For most careers, I suggest that women cut their hair to shoulder length or shorter in order to be taken more seriously in a business setting. Obviously this doesn't apply to actresses, ballet dancers, and others in fashion. But in more buttoned-down environments, a favorable impression is based on the ability to accomplish a goal within a given time period by drawing on mental power. The majority of such executives convey that power through their eyes. If your hair obscures your eyes, that's the first thing people will notice when they try to make eye contact. If you're trying to impress someone with your ability, you must try to deemphasize any distraction.

Our society is continually evolving, and our appearance is impacted by this process. We've gone from Renaissance wiggery to the highly styled curls of the 1940s to the unruly manes of the 1970s. Now we're in the computer age, and hair is going to become more streamlined and easier to care for. Quality and condition will be more important than complexity of style. The age of the weekly beauty parlor visit is over—we travel light, and put less emphasis on unnecessary folderol such as elaborate hairdos. Hair should form a halo around the face and be clean as a whistle, shiny as a china plate. It's your crowning glory. Health is reflected in the condition of your hair and gives people the subtle message that you're well and able. The only acceptable artificiality is the color enhancement men and women use to waylay the aging process or spruce up a dull natural shade.

When my clients become obstinate about cutting their hair, it tells me that they are inflexible in other ways. I told Connie that I didn't care whether she cut her hair, but strongly suggested she pull it away from her face. Women tend to wear their hair long during the interval between puberty and adulthood. Those who don't want to become self-reliant tend to draw on their physical charms to cover up insecurity about their intellect. At least if long hair is pulled back in a French braid or chignon, people have a clear view of the face. Men don't have hair in front of their ears; they expose their strong jaw lines. If women want to play in the same arena, they have to project a feminine version of the competence that a man's clean-cut look can convey.

Men, however, have their own ways of using hair to undermine their authority. Like Barry, the insurance executive in Chapter 1, bald men grow beards to tell the world that they are still virile. Some men who wear beards are trying to make a statement about their higher education and intellect. Instead, people see the beard and conclude that its wearer either teaches at a small college or, worse, belongs to a low socioeconomic group. Why? He's grooming himself less.

That's not all. Men who wear beards are by definition hiding a large part of their faces, which can make others think they're covering up something else. It doesn't matter whether that "something else" is a weak chin or something sinister about their character, the three-second impression has already been made.

Executive men visit the barber not just for frequent haircuts but also for eyebrow grooming. The area under the brow line should be clean, as well as the area between the brows, delineated by lining up a pencil or ruler alongside the nose. No single eyebrow line should grow unbroken across the face, and no visible hair should remain in ears or nose. Men often make the mistake of getting inexpensive haircuts when they'd look better if they went to a stylist. When in doubt about what's in vogue, look at pictures of models in magazine advertisements for a fair indication of the most current styling.

Scented colognes and aftershave lotions carry a potent message. No one should be able to smell you from three feet away, which means that, unless you're dealing with people who like to hug you, they shouldn't be able to smell you at all. This may seem obvious, but an awful lot of people make fools of themselves by overapplying a fragrance because they've become desensitized to its aroma. Speaking of lotions, there are new self-tanning lotions that simulate a healthy tan without subjecting your skin to the dangerous rays of the sun. After testing many of these products, I recommend Clarins of Paris because I found that their tanning treatments emit very little fragrance and yield the most natural-looking tan.

Time and weathering take their toll on everyone, so you may be ready for some cosmetic reconstruction to sustain your career. Top plastic surgeons like David Hidalgo, Sherrell Aston, and Robert Guida perform miracles on their patients with advanced techniques that require shorter recovery time.

Clothing

Once my clients have worked to balance their personality and adjust their point of view, I tell them it's time to package their message. I've helped them discover what kind of jewel they are, and we've polished off the rough edges. Now I must persuade them to present themselves in an appealing way.

Clients accept the notion that it's valuable to enhance their psychological awareness, but they still bristle at the notion that they should enhance their physical persona. We've all heard the familiar plaint, "Why shouldn't people accept me for my intellectual attributes, not my appearance?" I counter that being attractive isn't a detriment to the perception of a person's intellectual, moral, or ethical merits. After all, if someone can be induced to wear a distinctive suit or necktie to make a more favorable impression in order to get a $10,000 raise, why fight it?

Case Study: Nancy, 45

Here's an example of what a makeover and wardrobe can do to reinforce the attitudinal changes we're all trying to make. Nancy was the head of presentation graphics at an international consumer product company. She was overweight and unattractive, with a sharp tongue that intimidated her staff. In the company of her male superiors she was earthy and inappropriately flirtatious. The human resources director asked me to counsel her off-site because her abrasive temperament was causing interdepartmental problems. When we met, the first thing I noticed was her do-it-yourself dye job that nearly matched her multicolored wardrobe.

At first she was nearly impossible to deal with because she was so hostile, and paranoid about her overbearing boss. After I waded through her defenses, however, I found her to be a basically good-natured, bright individual who had buried her better qualities under a ton of personal garbage. Some of the problems I was called in to fix weren't even inherently negative. Nancy was a perfectionist who set high standards for herself and her colleagues; when her staff failed to meet those standards, she protected them by taking responsibility for their mistakes. Thus the group's output was low, and when things went wrong, the blame fell on Nancy.

In Nancy's case I had to work on her external persona before trying to reach her psyche. I decided to alter her appearance to elicit a favorable response from others which in turn would encourage her to improve her behavior. I set the tone for her transformation by taking her to a fashionable restaurant for lunch, then proceeded to a chic salon for a makeover. The colorist used a two-step process to transform her carrot-orange mop into an auburn mane. Then the makeup artist performed further miracles. He highlighted her eyes and eyebrows with neutral shades, brushed her cheeks with soft blush, and applied apricot lipstick. She happens to be very pretty but had been doing her best to hide it.

Next we headed for a department store, where I steered her toward some understated, classic suits. Nancy's wardrobe was a rainbow of colors, from clothing to shoes to handbags. Nothing was coordinated. I showed her that dressing monochromatically from head to toe can be a powerful look, especially when the outfit is accented with timeless leather shoes, handbag, and briefcase.

Nancy found that colleagues, acquaintances—even strangers—began to treat her more warmly, and she blossomed like a hothouse flower. I know some women might bristle at my suggestion that they should wear a bit of flattering makeup or find a fashionable hairstyle to make the best impression they can; it seems unfair that men have it a little easier when it comes to grooming. Interestingly, however, enhancing one's visual impression is less a matter of making a feminine statement than of taking appearance out of the equation. If cosmetics help you appear healthy and vibrant (as opposed to glamorous), others will be more receptive to your message—the substance of your presentation. Women who eschew makeup in an effort to be taken more seriously are actually leaving an impression that they lack self-esteem, not that they are intellectually superior.

Using her new political savvy, Nancy formed alliances, turning in-house rivals into supporters. Her group's improvement was so impressive that she was promoted and given a substantial raise.

Subsequently, Nancy was married and had a baby, and she believes that the work she did to change her outlook at the office is part of the reason she was able to achieve a more fulfilling personal life as well.

Clothing and manners aside, Nancy's story illustrates a point I made in the previous chapter: those who follow my program advance more than their careers, they enrich other people's lives. Nancy was just one of the people affected by her transformation; her colleagues now enjoy their work atmosphere more and her company is more prosperous. Nancy has the kind of visibility it takes to inspire others to fly with the eagles alongside her.

Wearing well-made classic clothing conveys the impression that you are centered, as it did with Nancy. For women, well-cut clothes create the illusion of power. You don't have to plunk down several thousand dollars for a designer suit—buy well-made knockoffs at department stores or find a dressmaker who will copy the look for you. It's better to take a cue from the French and spend your money on a few good outfits than to fill your closet with one-season impulse buys.

If, however, you're trying to make the leap clear to the top of the social triangle—the elite group I described in the last chapter—imitations won't vault you up there. That crowd can spot fake goods. They know, for example, that a real Cartier ''Tank'' watch band has a special retractable closing. When I was trying to show a client a significant difference between a designer suit and a less expensive copy, I held up a red wool jacket and asked her to tell me what was different about it. She stared blankly until I drew her attention to the shoulder line; it had no seam. The fabric was cut in one piece so that the sleeve flowed smoothly from wrist to neckline—a styling feature not easily duplicated in the copy.

Again, I'm not saying that the cut of a sleeve is important in the grand scheme of things—but it's a three-second signifier like a cashmere sweater. Only you can decide what level you are striving for. Just consider the impression you'll make, if, when in Rome, you do as the Romans do. Obviously not everyone's bank account is prepared for the expense of an entirely new wardrobe. But think of the investment that has already been made in your career—training school or college, perhaps graduate school, plus the time you've devoted to your work so far—and ask yourself whether it's worth a few designer outfits to complete your preparation for the career you aspire to have.

When searching for quality clothing, take note of the fabric, lining, cut, and accents such as buttons. All should look and feel luxurious and tailored with care. Women's pantsuits are okay in a creative environment; otherwise, a skirt is more appropriate. The hemline should be at or just above the knee so it falls gracefully when you are seated. Accentuate suits with luxurious silk scarfs artfully tied à la Hermès.

Men look especially powerful in custom-made suits of the finest woolens, tailored to their own silhouettes. However, the price may be too steep for your wallet, and you may decide to buy a well-made ready-to-wear suit. Play it safe by selecting one from a well-known men's store that carries quality merchandise. Off-price suits at discounters may not fit quite right, and so they aren't a real bargain. If you can, invest in custom-made shirts of Sea Island cotton with French cuffs and possibly a monogram. Check your workplace to see what the executives a few levels above you are wearing. No matter what your profession, either buy shirts without pockets or refrain from storing pens in your existing shirt pockets. A chief executive gives orders, he doesn't write them with his Montblanc pen. And unless you're a professor, button-down collars are déclassé.

Select belts of alligator or lizard, or try suspenders if they're appropriate at your workplace. But don't wear both at the same time—you'd be surprised how often that happens. The tie is like an arrow pointing up to its owner's face, so make it eye-catching. Hermès, Ferragamo, and Gucci use subtle colors in small patterns or subtle geometrics on luxurious silk to do the job; stores like Saks Fifth Avenue make nice imitations. Ambitious executives love to spend money on their neckties because it's the one place where they can really show off their unique personalities.

A final bit of advice about clothing: don't take Dress-Down Day too seriously. Whether your firm is one that has adopted "informal

Fridays'' or thrown out its dress code entirely, don't confuse ''informal'' with ''unkempt.'' An informal dress code means your clothes are more comfortable and less confining, not less stylish or put-together. Coordinated colors, proper fit, and fine fabrics are all still important. Anything that looks wash-and-wear is taboo, as are unironed cottons. Save jeans and khakis for the company picnic, along with athletic shoes. If you interpret a relaxed dress code to mean that you don't have to look polished, you may lose the ability to dress down altogether. Some companies have already determined that too many employees abuse these kinds of freedoms. Their answer is to eliminate them. The pendulum is beginning to swing back to less casual apparel if employees behave poorly.

Shoes

People think they can get away with a lot when it comes to their footwear, but they couldn't be more wrong. Shoes speak volumes, and the gatekeepers at certain levels of society listen to what they say. Good shoes announce, ''I care about myself. I buy only the finest quality''—a message you especially want to send when you're trying to impress a client or prospective employer.

Like the long pinkie nail Asian nobles once grew to demonstrate that they didn't have to perform any manual labor, fine footwear was worn by those whose lifestyle allowed them to go from limo to office and back again, avoiding puddle-jumping. Today, many business people wear butter-soft, wafer-thin, Italian loafers by Ferragamo and other designers. Fragile as these shoes are, it's not entirely a matter of fashion dictating to people. Tasseled loafers became acceptable when executives began traveling long distances on planes because they're easier to slip off and on than laced shoes. By the same token, canvas luggage came into vogue when there were no more porters. Practicality generally influences design.

Bankers still prefer sturdier cap-toed lace-ups; again, make your choice harmonious with your company's unique business atmosphere. As for socks, the most refined gentlemen emulate the Old Guard by wearing executive hose that cover the calf so no skin or hair is exposed when one crosses one's legs.

Like men, powerful women wear shoes they can walk in comfortably. Stiletto heels are passé for career climbers. In addition to being high-quality, women's pumps should always look conservative—and new. Styles by Ferragamo, Bally, Yves Saint Laurent, Charles Jourdan, and Bruno Magli are easily recognizable and are often copied by second-tier designers. Stockings are currently tonal semisheers like those worn by European women. No colored tights, please.

Toys

Don't forget the business accessories that declare your status. Examining your values can clue you in to the deeper aspects of your personality, like the fact that you prize recognition over money, but your values can also determine every choice you make about appearance. At some point a woman might have learned that she won't look pretty unless her calves are shown to best advantage in high heels; somewhere a man got the idea that he'd appear more intellectual if he grew a beard. Both have to shift their values before they can see why they insist on packaging themselves in a way that holds them back at the office.

To most people, a pen is a pen is a pen: disposable and interchangeable. But executives place a value on owning a pen worth using. Many a contract has been signed with a Cartier pen. Carrying around a signature pen is an interesting way to set yourself apart from the order-takers.

Handbags, like shoes, should look impeccable. Briefcases and tote bags should be crafted from the finest leather and have a seasoned appearance.

As for jewelry, a man should wear a watch, cuff links, and possibly a wedding band, period. The Concorde crowd wears Chaumet, Rolex, or Cartier, but a very good copy or a sporty Tag Heuer will suffice. Many male execs like to show off the level of their leisure pursuits by wearing unusual diving watches. When it comes to cuff links, it's better to own two pairs of real gold than ten pairs of gold-plated ones.

The same goes for women: a good trick to hide the fact that your mattress isn't stuffed with cash is to invest in a good watch and one signature item, like a heavy gold bracelet or a string of pearls. Earrings should sit on your earlobes, not dangle from them! Swinging earrings draw attention away from your face, not to mention the fact that it screams "party time." An unusual pin makes a nice statement and can serve as a nifty conversation starter at a conference or a party where you don't know many people. All someone has to do is express interest in your pin and you're instantly conversing about a neutral topic. (I'll offer more tips about the art of conversation later in this chapter.)

CHARM THE WORLD: POWER SECRET #6

Charm is the art of making other people feel comfortable on their own level without diminishing your standards of behavior. It enriches every room you enter and every person you encounter wherever you may be.

BODY LANGUAGE AND PUBLIC SPEAKING

Walk into a room, cross the floor, greet someone, shake his hand. Not three seconds have passed, but your body language has already fed him enough information to help him decide whether you're in his league. If your voice shifted into its upper register and your hands went clammy with nerves, you can be sure the impression you gave him was not one of power.

Here's a foolproof relaxation technique whose effects last about five minutes—long enough to ease into a new situation. Before the nerve-inducing event, stand outside the room. Close your eyes and clench your hands together so that every muscle in your system, from face to arms to hands to torso, becomes taut. Hold the clench so intensely that your muscles are shaking. After ten to twenty seconds, stop. However this magic works, it keeps the adrenaline from driving you into a panic state for that vital five-minute interval.

Composure achieved, it's time to walk into the room with authority and poise. Shoulders back, spine erect, movements smooth, and always, always a friendly smile. Shake hands firmly, thumb joint to thumb joint. No knuckle-crunchers or limp wrists, please. Look directly at the other person throughout the encounter.

Keep your voice in its lower register and speak at a moderate pace to communicate confidence and ease. The higher up the chain of command, the slower one speaks. Neophytes tend to talk at a rapid-fire pace because they fear they'll be cut off before they can finish. Worse, they finish statements with an upward inflection, as though asking a question. The effect: they sound doubtful and submissive.

Executives take their time when they address a group; they do this to ensure a captive audience. What they have to say is important, and as long as they speak with authority, no one dares to interrupt. There is an exception to this rule: Northeasterners, especially New Yorkers, speak more quickly than people from other parts of the United States. Some Yankees find it takes a little patience to follow a Southerner's leisurely drawl.

There is an optimal speed; people will be most attentive and able to comprehend your message if you speak at a rate of roughly 175 words per minute.

I can't tell you the number of people I meet who are held back because of an unpleasant way of speaking. Even someone with a doctorate will come across as uneducated if he speaks with a strong regional accent. The son of one of the wealthiest families in South America failed to win a gig as a TV news broadcaster because his beautiful, musical accent was so thick, he swallowed his words. A few sessions with a language coach could have smoothed out his delivery. Of course, there are exceptions to this rule, and I certainly don't mean to say that everyone has to speak like a generic sitcom character in order to get ahead. But the way to make doors swing open is to follow a strict code of behavior—it's the people who make it to the top who can improvise. The finest companies won't even hire support staff who can't speak proper English. After all, they're the ones who are interfacing with the public, and the impression they make is the one outsiders have of the company itself.

Compulsive habits make people look undisciplined and neurotic. I have known clients who don't even realize they are constantly playing with their hair. People who pick at their fingers betray their tension. One man touched his lip as he spoke, obscuring the view of his mouth and diluting the power of his words. Inserting "uh" or "um" between thoughts makes it seem as if the person can't think silently, or is unwilling to allow someone else to break into the conversation. Gesticulating to excess makes people look like nervous chickens flapping their wings.

ARTFUL CONVERSATION

Everyone wonders how to begin a conversation. The most genteel way to converse with new people, whether in business or social settings, is by using an indirect approach. The most off-putting question you can ask a sophisticated person you don't know well is: "What do you do?" Most of us try that conversation starter within minutes of meeting someone in order to get to know him or her better. But foreigners think it terribly intrusive, and since manners become more refined in higher status levels, executives think it's pretty flatfooted too. Here's my personal hit list.

THE TEN MOST INAPPROPRIATE QUESTIONS

1. What do you do for a living?

2. Where are you from?

3. Where did you go to school?

4. Where do you live?

5. How did you meet so-and-so?

6. Where did you buy that/how much did you pay for it?

7. What do you think of your company/boss?

8. Whom are you going to vote for?

9. What religion are you?

10. Are you married/how old are your children?

A lot of people reading this list might wonder what is left to talk about, but it's not as difficult as it may seem. These questions are distinctly American—in most other countries, people consider such lines of inquiry far too personal for conversation among casual acquaintances or business associates. Besides the fact that these questions can be offensive, they don't actually achieve intimacy between strangers. In fact, they can do just the opposite—break any bridge you were trying to build. If you ask someone where he lives and find that you come from opposite ends of town, where do you go from there? What if that means you come from the wrong side of the tracks and he comes from the right side? You haven't exactly established a bond.

If you keep asking questions and the other person is too polite to ask them right back, he may get the feeling you're sizing him up to figure out if he's someone you can take advantage of. In the junior society set of New York, Rome, London, or Paris, the scions of wealthy families can spot so-called "jumps," or social climbers, by the number of personal questions they ask. In this crowd, the query most likely to get an interloper kicked out is: "What do your parents do?"

I usually try to focus on a current topic of interest, something abstract and noninvasive. Choose a subject so broad in scope that your responses can't be seen as judgmental. Make casual statements that aren't too heavy, and don't ask probing questions. The three topics that always work—banal as they may seem—are the weather, transportation, and forthcoming sports events. You just can't get in trouble talking about Wimbledon, or the new airport in Denver that's twenty miles from anywhere, or the unseasonable temperature. These subjects can launch you into a worthwhile conversation, or at least give you enough information to move safely to a line of discussion that's of interest to your partner.

Once the conversation moves on, continue to be cautious. Don't offer information about yourself unless you're sure it will be well received. It might seem nonthreatening to talk about a movie or an opera, but the minute you get into cultural topics you're expressing opinions, and that's how the fragile bonds of fresh acquaintance can be broken. Even introducing humor is a dicey proposition: how can you be sure the person has a sense of humor? About the only way you can humanize the conversation is to talk about a celebrity.

Let's say you've seen the same person at three parties in a row or at a few business functions and you want to move the association to a deeper level. There are ways to get answers to the questions I listed above. The easiest one is to offer information about yourself, which prompts others to fill in the blanks about themselves. Another way is to make a statement that surrounds the question with an observation or a compliment. Both are ways of sharing and prompting the other person to share. Here are the noninvasive approaches to use instead of the conversation-killers above. Remember, these aren't alternative ways to pump a new acquaintance. These are meant to help you go deeper after a few auspicious meetings.

NONINVASIVE COMMENTS

1. I imagine you've got a really interesting career.

2. Nobody seems to come from (fill in name of town you're in) anymore.

3. You look like a Middlebury graduate to me.

4. I've been trying to make up my mind whether to move to the suburbs and commute.

5. There must be some link that brings us to the same events.

6. That's an intriguing pin. (Never ever ask the price or source of an object, and don't offer that information, either. He didn't compliment your jewelry, he complimented your taste.)

7. Your job sounds complex.

8. The candidates running for election really present a challenge this year.

9. There are so many philosophies and spiritual beliefs out there, I wish I understood them all better.

10. Your children must be terrific athletes.

Introductions

A vital part of conversing is making proper introductions. The etiquette is easy if you remember to address the senior person first. For example, "Mr. Exec, may I introduce Ann Coleman, who is one of my clients?" followed by, "Anne, this is Bob Exec, the head of our agency." In less formal settings, it is all right to begin using first names, especially after suggesting it: "Bob, this is Anne Coleman, a client of mine." "Anne, this is Bob Exec, our founder."

TABLE ETIQUETTE

Everyone smirks when I bring up the subject of table manners, but you can tell more about people by their table manners than by any other single trait. It comes up in business all the time, and not just at client lunches. When your second interview for a big job was scheduled as a lunch, did you think your potential employer was rewarding you for being one of his top candidates? Hardly. He wanted to observe your table manners, to see if you could hold your own with the big boys (and girls). And if he asked you to bring along your spouse, he wanted to make sure that he or she wouldn't derail your business deals by eating with elbows on the table.

The vice-chairman of a food industry conglomerate, whom I'll call Richard, had bought Peter's smaller food service company and was debating how much power to give Peter in the organization. Richard asked me to help him decide whether he should make Peter president of the new division. We took Peter to a beautiful restaurant for dinner, and after we observed his atrocious table manners, Richard made Peter a vice-president instead. The fact that he couldn't eat properly meant he wasn't familiar with the level of protocol necessary for such a prominent position.

Having gracious table manners is a definite asset that distinguishes you from the usual bunch of rude characters. At the highest levels of business, executives use the Continental dining style—holding the fork in the left hand and the knife in the right without switching American-style. A few years ago when I was preparing twenty senior executives from a Fortune 500 company for an upcoming conference with their firm's leading clients, I opened a session by giving each participant a robin's-egg-blue Tiffany box wrapped with a white bow. You should have seen the bewildered expressions when the executives unwrapped their presents and found copies of Walter Hoving's *Tiffany's Table Manners for Teenagers* inside.

What if you've been told all your life that it's gauche to eat without switching hands? Fine, then don't change. As the saying goes, the only person who ever really wants a change is a wet baby. But if you're trying to expand your horizons or advance your career, and you intend to spend the rest of your life in that world, remember that the purpose of displaying manners is to make others comfortable. People who travel in international circles use the Continental method of dining. To make them comfortable, you must eat the way they do.

To many middle-class Americans, Continental manners actually look less refined. I believe that's because centuries ago immigrants with roots in England dined in the Continental manner, and the new American pioneers tried to distance themselves from that group. The rationale behind Continental dining is that it requires less bodily movement. Small bits of food pushed onto the back of the fork mean smaller bites, thus minimizing the action of dining, and turning the focus of the meal to socializing. You're not supposed to gain attention with your arms and hands, you're supposed to draw on your charm. There's nothing charming about passing your knife from hand to hand and scooping large portions of food into your mouth. If you still question which is the gold standard today, look to Tiffany, the arbiter of taste and style in the United States.

Essentially, Walter Hoving emphasizes the fact that no one is at a social meal for the nourishment. It is considerate to wait until everyone is served before taking a bite of food. Once you have started eating, pace yourself so that you finish at the same time as your host—he, after all, is orchestrating the evening. When eating bread, tear off small, bite-sized pieces before adding butter, and always pass the salt and pepper as a unit and place them in front of the next diner. Many rituals stem from superstitions; it's considered bad luck to hand anyone salt, so we neutralize the effect by passing pepper at the same time. Continental manners dictate keeping your hands visible on the table at all times. This tradition found its source in medieval Europe when being unable to see your dining partner's hands meant he could stab you under the table at any moment.

INTERNATIONAL PROTOCOL

Business people abroad follow centuries-old traditions that must be acknowledged before transactions begin. An understanding of cultural differences and nuances will smooth your way and prevent embarrassing slip-ups. Even something as simple as shaking hands in greeting may not be appropriate in countries where it is taboo to be touched. Americans tend to be casual, using first names in business and treating even the newest of contacts with familiarity. This behavior is bewildering to people from virtually every other nation on earth.

Americans have a reputation for being egocentric, but that doesn't mean *you* have to be. It helps to be cognizant of two factors while conducting business with a foreigner: the rituals of his country and his rank. Even if you pay close attention, it's impossible to follow every tradition flawlessly, but demonstrating that you've made the effort is often enough to keep relations on the right track. A good source for study is *Kiss, Bow, or Shake Hands,* by Terri Morrison, Wayne A. Conaway, and George Borden, Ph.D., from which some of the information later in this chapter is drawn.

Outside the United States, never use a first name without an invitation; it's highly improper. It may be offered after you establish a long association, but don't hold your breath. Even staff members address their superiors by their last names as a sign of respect. Receptionists treat callers with the same civility, unlike some of their counterparts here—those gum-cracking wonders who behave as if you are a personal friend by immediately using your given name.

You would be stunned by how strictly people in other countries hold to class distinctions. If you don't show the same deference, you could do yourself out of a deal. Regardless, the deal making

will have to wait until you've broken bread. International companies believe it is important to entertain a guest so as to establish
rapport before beginning a transaction. It's also an excuse to ply
you with liquor in an effort to loosen your tongue. When dinner
begins, you are expected to partake of whatever the host serves,
even if that includes raw fish in Japan, bear paw soup in China,
escargots in France, salad served after the main course, and fire-
water throughout.

Wherever you are, from your boss's office to the Taj Mahal,
think of yourself as playing an endless game of Mother-May-I.
Wait for your host's cues before using the phone or borrowing a
pen. The game must progress quite far indeed before you take the
giant step of serving him—or yourself—when you're in his territory (such as pouring coffee for both of you when you visit his
office). Don't walk around with a sense of entitlement, as if you
were royalty. Leave every place better than you found it; leave
every person enriched for having interacted with you.

Asia

Be hyperconscious of local rituals. The highest-ranking member of
your team should enter the meeting first, and subordinates mustn't
interrupt their superiors. Greet business people with a bow, dipping
especially low if you're meeting a higher-ranking officer. If you
proffer a business gift, know that a Chinese recipient may decline it
three times before accepting. Play along by insisting he accept, and
when he does, thank him. No business will be conducted until you
drink tea with your Asian counterparts—which you won't do until
your host drinks first, of course.

Rituals aren't the only differences you'll encounter. Written Chinese has no verb tenses other than the present, so expect to add a
lot of words like "tomorrow" and "last year" to your contract to
avoid confusion. Both written and spoken Japanese have four levels
of deference, making it easy to offend a company officer by ad-
dressing him incorrectly. I recently opened an annual report published by the Aeon Group in Japan, and was amazed to discover a
section titled, "Lessons in Japanese Etiquette." This international

conglomerate, which owns Talbot's, stated: "The mark of a well-educated Japanese is the ability to communicate politely in the appropriate situation. The relative age and social position between the speakers, such as a boss and subordinate, a salesperson and customer, or two friends, will indicate the politeness required."

In Japan, it is distasteful for other people to see dirt on the soles of anyone's shoes, so it is courteous to slip shoes off at the door. In fact, in most European countries, you will appear more refined and well grounded if you keep both feet flat to the floor.

A famous incident occurred when Russian President Nikita Khrushchev met with Richard Nixon. During the meeting, Khrushchev crossed his legs and casually turned up his foot, revealing a big hole in the sole of his shoe. The international press had a field day, chastising Khrushchev for his faux pas. Even the editors of the *New York Times* scolded him for his bad manners. So, if you do choose to cross your legs, raise one leg up far enough to be able to lock it over the other so both legs will form one powerful line with soles out of sight. It's easier to do this if you are slim. Remember to keep both feet parallel, with your toes pointed in the same direction. This rule holds whether you are standing or sitting with your legs crossed. (In portraits of royal families, virtually every member of the group is sitting precisely this way.) Crossing your legs properly won't ensure a good impression, however, if you're a man wearing ankle socks that don't cover the leg—you'll look just like a turkey! A woman wearing a particularly short skirt should put both feet on the floor, knees together; in this case, crossing her legs would reveal too much of her thigh.

During meals, never talk when you have food in your mouth. The appearance of an open mouth is so repugnant to an Asian that he covers his mouth as he sips his tea or takes a bite of food. Asians find Westerners who sneeze, blow their noses, or yawn during dinner offensive.

In China, the need to maintain an appearance of harmony can work against Americans, who tend to lose their heads during negotiations and think nothing of it. The Chinese will use this to their advantage, dragging out talks past your deadline to put themselves in a more favorable position. Better not to discuss your deadline at all. Throughout Asia, business people will continue to renegotiate a supposedly final contract. At no time should you allow your frustration to make you say something that will cause your counterpart to lose face.

In Hong Kong, don't take the word "yes" to mean that your business partner agrees with you. It just means he understands what you are saying. He'll never say no, just that your proposal would be very challenging. In Japan, negative questions receive the opposite response to what an American would expect. If, for example, you say, "Don't you want to try this approach?" and your Japanese acquaintance says, "Yes," he means you're right—he doesn't want to try your approach.

Avoid using extreme facial expressions or hand gestures. The Chinese don't use their hands when they speak, so your movements will only distract them. In Japan, every motion has a meaning, so your face and hands will convey messages you may not intend.

Throughout Asia, it is considered impolite not to hand a business card upon introduction, and very insulting not to be given your card in return. Never pass your business card with your left hand. It is the custom to present your business card with both hands, thumbs on the upper corners of the card so it is easily readable by the recipient. Your title has more meaning than your name because your level of power is important in Eastern culture.

Treat any card you receive as if it were precious. That means you can't slip it into your back pocket, or even into a wallet that ends up in a back pocket.

While visiting Asia, female executives should be especially careful about their behavior. It is a sad fact that they simply are not treated as equals by Asian businessmen. They should dress, speak, and act conservatively, and refuse alcohol. A woman who wears bangs will be considered lower class, so she should consider styling her hair in a way that will reveal her forehead. Men with hair on their faces will be similarly dismissed—shave that beard!

South America

American impatience is extremely distasteful to many South Americans. Meetings begin late and progress at a leisurely pace. Greetings and partings go on and on, including as many as three kisses between women (married women get only two; the third is to wish a single woman good luck in finding a husband). At business meals, deals aren't discussed until coffee is served. In all countries, research hand motions and signs of mourning to avoid making major gaffes—in Brazil our sign for okay is considered vulgar, and gifts in black and purple signify death.

Great Britain

We speak the same language, but not all words have the same meaning. Most of us know many of these differences, such as "loo" for toilet and "boot" for the trunk of a car. But in business it helps to know that, when an Englishman "tables" a discussion, it means he starts it rather than putting it off until later. A pitch that "bombed" has triumphed rather than failed disastrously.

Unlike ours, Britain is not a litigious society, and their business people can be insulted by our insistence on attorneys (solicitors). Oral agreements are considered binding, and contracts don't go to lawyers unless they're especially complicated. If necessary, use a British attorney to sort out the elements of your deal.

In Britain, as in Europe, control your impulse to ask blunt questions of the "What do you do?" variety. Europeans consider these questions to be especially personal. Try the alternatives listed on page 109 instead.

France

France, like England, doesn't depend on attorneys to the extent we do. In France it's because of the civil law system. Commercial agreements need only refer to the legal code, allowing many savvy business people to write their own contracts.

Many of the mistakes American executives make in France involve etiquette. If you are fortunate enough to be entertained in someone's home, wait for the hostess or a servant to pass the hors d'oeuvre. Don't walk over and help yourself to more—you have to wait until they are passed again. Frenchmen shudder when the cheese course is served and they watch Americans cut off the tip on a wedge of Brie instead of cutting at an angle, as if it were a piece of pie.

Europeans dislike any personal discussion of money and find fault with people from the States who constantly speak about the cost of things. But you knew better than to do that anyway!

Germany

Germans tend to live up to their reputation for being closed and regimented. They don't even keep their colleagues informed about the details of your deal. Therefore your contact is the only person you should ever speak to. Add this lack of intracompany communications to their slow and steady work ethic, and you get a country whose business deals take forever. So be patient.

If you arrive even one minute late to a meeting with a German businessman, he'll be quite insulted. Humor won't dig you out of your hole; Germans think business is serious. Document your every claim with reams of data, and eliminate hyperbole from your conversation. Eliminate business from breakfast, too—Germans dislike breakfast meetings.

Middle East

In most parts of the Middle East, the left hand is considered unclean, so you should gesticulate, eat, and pass your business card with the right hand only, even if you're left-handed. Expect to be greeted with a lot of physical contact and to be spoken to at an uncomfortably close distance.

Muslims in Saudi Arabia, like the Sikhs in India, want to break bread and drink tea with you before they show any interest in your sales presentation. A powerful bond will be forged during a meal if you answer their questions with lengthy and flattering answers. A typical conversation might go like this.

"How was your flight to my country?"

A wise response would be: "It was impressive to fly over Saudi Arabia, the cradle of civilization and the home of the kingdom of Islam, where Mecca is."

In Saudi Arabia, it is customary to keep less influential and foreign business people waiting, although you should arrive on time yourself. Once the Saudis arrive, the meeting will begin slowly, with exchanges such as the one above being common. After the meeting is over, a decision will be a long time in coming. A lot of "yessing" at the end of the meeting may have led you to believe you had a deal, but that's part of their politesse.

Women aren't permitted to engage in business in many countries of the Middle East, and they are not included at business events. When you are making small talk before a meeting begins, you will be wise not to make any comments about a businessman's wife or family.

Saudis expect you to keep your feet on the floor at all times. The sole of a person's shoe touches dirt, so it is considered bad form to display it. And, speaking of body language, don't give him the American "thumbs up." It's considered indecent.

THREE-SECOND OVERVIEW

You've learned about protocol and the packaging required around the globe. Now it's time to prepare to market yourself. In the next chapter, I'll show you what it takes to launch a successful campaign.

6

Marketing Yourself to the Company

Minefields abound in the workplace, from politically charged staff meetings to sticky salary negotiations. I can show you how to maneuver through them without triggering an explosion, but first you have to get in the door. Whether this is your first job or your twenty-first, whether you're unemployed or unsatisfactorily employed, a fulfilling career begins with a sensational résumé.

UNABASHED SELF-PROMOTION: POWER SECRET #7

You can't win the election if you vote for the other guy. Playing John Alden is out of style. Marketing yourself is like marketing a product. Your full name is your logo. Your expertise is a precious commodity. Your persona is added value. Your packaging is your marketing approach. Remember, a good salesman never knocks the product.

WINNING RÉSUMÉS

Forget everything you've been taught about résumé writing. That includes using active verbs, full sentences, and specific employment dates for past jobs. This is a new era. Your résumé is a press release whose purpose is to publicize a hot new product: you. Like a magazine designed to fly off the stands, today's résumé grabs the reader with enticing headlines, currency figures, and percentages. Take a look at the following examples, one of which is a résumé makeover, and then I'll tell you what makes them different from the usual ho-hum form.

DENISE COLEMAN

123 Waterside Drive, Chicago, Illinois 76543
312 001 1111

SUMMARY

Broad experience in leasing and selling corporate real estate with major firms with a proven record of sales and tenant services. Searching for opportunity to apply extensive experience in an aggressive profit-oriented company.

EXPERIENCE

ASSET REPRESENTATIVE
BIG NAME PROPERTIES, INC.   1988 to present

At Cityside Center, I was employed by one of the top ten developers in the United States as an owners' representative with respect to the leasing of various commercial properties in the Chicago area. Reporting to the President. Responsible for leasing and tenant activity in approximately 3 million square feet.

At Longview Park, I participated in primary negotiations for the largest lease transaction in Evanston, Illinois: Fish Associates, 90,000 sq. feet; and the second largest lease transaction in Chicago: Princeville Plaza, 1,700,000 sq. ft. in 1989.

This transaction entailed a take-back of a lease for two of the three buildings in the suburban office park. I negotiated the terms of both lease transactions and dealt with the existing subtenants in the other building to remain on a direct basis.

In the Priceville Plaza transaction, I negotiated an initial lease of 500,000 sq. ft. with options expanding the occupancy over 20 years.

Additionallly, I coordinated the electrical and mechanical engineers for the tenants with the building engineers to successfully conclude that aspect of the transaction.

REAL ESTATE BROKER
JONES, JONES, & JONES, Inc.   1984 - 1988

Active in subleasing approximately 75,000 sq. ft. for Creative Advertising Corp. and acted as the leasing agent for Read More Books Building and 545 Michigan Avenue. Planned and implemented a marketing effort for available space. Budgeted annually each building's leasing activity, working closely with accounting and building management.

REAL ESTATE SALESPERSON
BIG CHEESE SALES & LEASING CORP.   1982 - 1984

Represented tenants in leasing offices, showrooms, and retail store mall space. Clients included: Faded Jeans, Emelio Veneto, and Speedy Car Rental.

EDUCATION

Western Rodeo University,   1980
Ivy League School of Business,   1982

Before and After

The résumé Denise Coleman submitted to me is all too typical; notice that it's typewritten and uses paragraphs to describe her work experience. As you'll see, her résumé is perfectly competent, but it won't land her a dream job.

Compare Denise's original résumé with the new version shown on page 122. Since she's in real estate, I've listed the names of the buildings whose leases she's completed, as well as the square footage of the spaces. The reader's eye is pulled down the page, jumping from name to number, name to number. This method has freed up enough space to incorporate all of the information on one page.

DENISE COLEMAN

123 Waterside Drive, Chicago, Illinois 76543 * 312 001 1111

REAL ESTATE SALES EXECUTIVE

NEGOTIATE LEASES   REPRESENT TENANTS
LEASING AGENT   MARKET SERVICES

ASSET REPRESENTATIVE

BIG NAME PROPERTIES, INC.   1988 to present
Report to President

LEASE COMMERCIAL PROPERTY

Cityside Center - 3,000,000 sq. ft.

Market and close initial retail lease transactions to prestigious clients
i.e. Jade Cosmetics, Bingo's Copy Center
Coordinate existing tenant expansions

Princeville Plaza - 1,700,000 sq. ft.

$000M deal - second largest lease in Chicago in 1989
Designed twenty-year tenant expansion plan - 500,000 to 1,000,000 sq. ft.
Coordinated technical advisers; lawyers, brokers, engineers, contractors

Longview Park - 300,000 sq. ft.

90,000 sq. ft. - largest lease in Evanston, Illinois in 1990
Represented Fish Associates in taking over Acme's leasehold
Re-leased the property to Lightbulb Corporation

REAL ESTATE BROKER

JONES, JONES, & JONES, INC.   1984 - 1988
Report to President and Chairman

SUBLEASING CONSULTANT   75,000 sq. ft. Creative Advertising Corp.

LEASING AGENT   400,000 sq. ft. Read More Books Building

150,000 sq. ft. 545 Michigan Avenue

20,000 sq. ft. 100 River Drive

REAL ESTATE SALES, Assistant Vice President

BIG CHEESE SALES & LEASING CORP.   1982 - 1984
Report to Vice President

REPRESENTED TENANTS IN LEASE TRANSACTIONS

Faded Jeans, Inc., Emilio Veneto, Speedy Car Rental among others

EDUCATION

Western Rodeo State University   1980

Ivy League School of Business   1982

Jane Doe's revised résumé puts her titles, direct reports, and dollar figures at the left side of the page, where the reader will quickly key in on them. The dates of her tenure at each company are listed at the right, but the specific years she held each position within the company are omitted; Jane can discuss specifics during the actual interview.

J A N E   D O E

5 West Charming Street   *   New York, NY   *   212 555. 6789 Home

MARKETING & MERCHANDISING EXECUTIVE

MAJOR RETAILER   *1999 - present*

SENIOR VICE PRESIDENT
Report to Chairman of Special Merchandising Office

  $000M annually at retail - Women's Apparel

- 00 divisions: Sweaters; Blouses; Blazers; Skirts; Pants
- 00 countries researched for cost effective merchandise to increase profit margins
- 00 international buying trips organized for executives
- 00 national executives directed to internationally acquire private label merchandise
- 00 major product maketing campaigns; packaging and sales promotion materials
- 00 motivational sales training seminars, including interactive televised broadcasts

GROUP VICE PRESIDENT
Reported to President of Special Merchandise

  $000M Designer Sportswear

  00 divisions
  Introduced international prestige sportswear line
  Launched $00M boutique program, including packaging and promotional materials

MERCHANDISING ADMINISTRATOR
Reported to Senior Vice President

  $00M private label placements - Young Men's Athletic Wear

  Introduced first national private label sneaker program

ANOTHER MAJOR RETAILER   *1987 - 1999*

ASSISTANT STORE MANAGER

  $00M annual volume - 5 catagories

  Managed 00 selling associates, including 00 executives

BUYER

  $0M annual volume

  Produced 00% profit annually

SALES MANAGER

  $0M annual volume

EDUCATION

  BS University of the Sea - Honors, 1987

  Graduate Degree Preparation - Prestigious University, 1990 - 1993

John Jones was uncomfortable abandoning the time-honored tradition of filling a résumé with action verbs, so I showed him a way to use the verbs to lead into numbers and figures quantifying his successes. Readers who skip past words to search for dollar figures can find them easily; the typeface as well as the space between the verbs and the numbers sets them apart.

JOHN JONES

*3 Lover's Lane * Town, CA 06820 * 714 555 1234 H * 714 555 5678 O*

BUSINESS DEVELOPMENT

*EXECUTION * DEVELOPMENT * RESTRUCTURING * DIVESTITURE*

BAY CITY RESEARCH, INC.   1986 to present

PRIVATE INVESTMENTS - companies with revenues up to $000 million

Developed	0 companies - served as a board member; wrote business plans; streamlined staffs; restructured financings; completed refinancings
Managed	0 company turnarounds - on site
Directed	0 new investments, up to $00M, from initial opportunities to closing
Structured	0 new investments
Negotiated	0 initial public offerings
Attracted	0 investors for capital investment, ultimately $00M profit
Sold	0 subsidiaries; 0 divisions; 0 equity interests

BANK OF THE WORLD   1982 - 1986

NEW BUSINESS DEVELOPMENT

Generated	$0.0 million in fees in a highly competiteve market, during 1985
Syndicated	$000 million secured loan to a savings and loan
Managed	$000 million mortgage banking portfolio
Established	European bank relationships - Holland, France, Great Britain,
Assisted	Project X - Peruvian Loan Restructuring
Graduate	Executive Training Program

EDUCATION

B.A.	University of the North	1980
	President, Northern Athletic Association	
	Fancy Dan Academy	1976
	Senior Year in France	

Languages	Fluent in French, German, Dutch

How to Do It

The most important information on a résumé is your *name*, not the word "résumé." This may seem obvious, but many inexperienced job seekers put that word in bold letters right at the top of the page, followed by redundant headings such as "work experience." Type your name in capital letters at the top—remember, it's the name of the product you're selling. Eliminate the ever popular "objective" line that usually follows the candidate's name. It's unnecessary. The person you're trying to influence doesn't care about your objective, he cares about his own needs. Instead, substitute two or three flash words defining your expertise. These qualifiers focus the reader's attention on your attributes and determine his three-second impression of your résumé. Recent graduates can use this headline to indicate their desire to work in an analytical, creative, technical, administrative, or sales capacity, to name a few.

When writing your résumé, remember this stark reality: few people actually *read* a résumé, they skim it. But they can be depended on to read the first and last lines of almost any document, so these should include a job hunter's most important material. At the top, the résumé writer's specialty attracts the reader's eye. At the bottom, don't put information about your personal interests (tennis, bingo, butterfly collecting)—instead, cite your most impressive award or affiliation. Keep the interviewer focused on your skills, not your hobbies.

There's another reason to eliminate the section about personal interests: It violates the principles of psychodynamics I've outlined in this book. When you meet with an interviewer, you're trying to build a bridge between the two of you so that he will recommend you for the job. Unless you are extremely familiar with the details of his personal life, you risk alienating him by giving him information that breaks the bond you've established. Say you enjoy hunting and he's a member of an animal protection society? Or you're an avid golfer and he feels threatened by country club types? Or you've won a half dozen bowling trophies and he considers bowlers to be lower-class? Better to elicit his prejudices in the course of the interview and give yourself the room to tailor your approach on the spot.

Notice how airy the sample résumés are, how uncluttered the pages? This look invites the reader in and assures him he doesn't have to slog through long paragraphs to assess your worth. Moreover, if you've changed jobs often, you can put yourself in a better light by composing a "skills résumé" that emphasizes your abilities before listing the companies where you've worked. It may help to have the following list of skills in front of you as you condense your old résumé into this format. After selecting a skill word, follow it with your own specific area of expertise, such as, writing advertising copy.

Skill Words

Inventing	Designing
Building	Writing
Editing	Planning
Organizing	Managing
Selling	Researching
Appraising	Negotiating
Auditing	Distributing

Notice that the list doesn't include words like "implementing"—words people don't actually use in ordinary conversation. In addition, I'll get the vapors if you use the phrase "responsible for" anywhere. Space-waster words and phrases have no place in a sleek, paragraphless résumé.

Using the list of skill words as a guide, quantify and qualify your work history, as Jane Doe did, with the specific numbers and percentages of your accomplishments. Make clear your importance and level of power within the company. Keep in mind that Western society reads from left to right, so eye-catching numbers or percentages should be placed at the left to show solid results and capture the reader's attention. Relegate the dates of employment to the right side of the page, using years only unless you have very little experience. You can fill in the details during your interview.

In certain industries, the title or level of responsibility is paramount and deserves a place of honor along the left side of the page. Executive recruiters are often interested in the chain of command, since the meaning of a particular title can vary widely from company to company. Thus, it can help to include the title of the manager you report to. Even the names of the companies you've worked for need this sort of classification, detailing their annual sales or market status to show where they rank within their industries. Unlike applying to college, there's no SAT score to help employers compare job candidates on a level playing field.

After work history and achievements come education, including awards, associations, and community or philanthropic activities if applicable. Prune your descriptions mercilessly—the more print on the page, the more defensive you seem. Think of former United States President Jimmy Carter. Type the following words on a piece of paper and you'd be done:

> Diplomat at-large
> Former President of the United States
> Former Governor of Georgia
> Peanut plantation owner
> Graduate of Annapolis

Note that his résumé has just five lines and there's no question of the dimension of Carter's power.

Vary both the type size and the font, as on a newspaper page, to sustain the reader's interest. Times Roman generally looks best; but don't hesitate to include italic and boldface. I suggest to my clients that they include a border, called a tombstone, which may enhance the look of the page and catch the reader's eye. Try yours with and without a border to see if it makes a difference.

Edit the résumé down to one page, then expand it to two pages if you can boast an exceptional number of awards and affiliations that deserve their own sheet. The third page is for references, which you supply only when asked. Don't type "references available upon request" at the bottom of the résumé—it's unnecessary. Create the résumé on a computer and print it out on good-quality white or cream-colored paper using a laser printer. (Don't roll your eyes—

you'd be surprised how many people still use a typewriter to produce their résumés.) If you don't have access to a computer and laser printer, it's worth spending the money to have someone print a professional-looking résumé for you.

KNOW YOUR INTERVIEWER

You don't need to give someone a values test in order to divine his point of view. There are means of indirect discovery that will help you put together enough information about the interviewer to gain some control over your interaction. Here's a partial list worth checking out through friends, contacts, recruiters, etc.

Biography
    Company, title, or level of power
    Experience
    Education
    Approximate age
    Nationality
    Religion
    Marital and family status
Outside interests
    Sports
    Literature
    Cultural events
    Travel
Preferences
    Food
    Music
    Apparel
    Automobile
Pride and prejudices
    Politics
    Gender
    Competitiveness

Almost any easily obtained public information can help you construct a profile of the person to whom you want to tailor a presentation, whether it be a potential boss or the board members of a private club you'd like to join. If your interviewer accepted a lower-paying position at the same level as his previous job but at a more prestigious company, eventual advancement and exposure might have been more important to him than being a big fish in a small pond. If he once moved from the public sector to a private company, money may be more of a priority for him than altruistic deeds. In the latter case, rambling in your interview about the importance of self-sacrifice and good works will only strike a nerve and close off his receptivity to you.

THE INTERVIEW

Arrive fifteen minutes early; besides assuring punctuality, the extra time gives you the chance to compose yourself before the meeting begins. Ask to use the lavatory—it might be located near a work area where you'll have the opportunity to observe the employees' demeanor and their working environment. The condition of the lavatory itself is revealing; I've visited dozens of companies that have beautiful lobbies and reception areas while the employees' lavatories are one step above outdoor plumbing. This should give some indication of how the company treats its workers.

Following the guidelines in Chapter 5, wear the appropriate costume for the world you'd like to enter. That might include a stylish yet conservative haircut and manicure (men take note!), a fountain pen, and a quality briefcase or leather folder. Greet your interviewer with a friendly smile, direct eye contact, and a firm handshake.

Graciously inquire how long the interview will last so you can cover key topics in the allotted time. Then engage the interviewer in ice-breaking small talk as you exchange business cards. Build mutual respect before starting your presentation by drawing on your research to comment on company activities.

If you've done a background check on your interviewer, you've already made an educated guess about his personality type and noted how to tailor your approach to suit his communication style. Perhaps you know something about his values and socioeconomic background as discussed in Chapters 3 and 4. The outcome of the interview may be a mystery to you, but the interviewer isn't—or shouldn't be. If you've done your homework, you've learned enough about him to modify your approach so that, by the time the interview has ended, he doesn't think his department can go forward without you!

At all times, try to build bridges, not create gaps. Use the lawyer's technique of not asking any question to which you don't already know the answer. For example, John Job Hunter shouldn't boast about winning scholarships and working two jobs to put himself through community college unless he knows Ira Interviewer has a similar background. Ira might have gone to an Ivy League school—all expenses paid—and he'll look down his nose at John's working-class background.

The beauty of a values assessment is that it makes it possible to relate to anyone, no matter how little common ground there seems at first to exist between you. In the previous example, John wouldn't lie and say he went to Yale. Instead, he would emphasize the interests he and Ira share. If Ira asked about John's college experience, and John had found out that both he and Ira played football for their university teams, he might mention how much he enjoyed it. If he concluded from the values assessment that Ira is motivated by objective results, John would talk about his accomplishments in terms of how much profit they brought to his companies rather than how satisfied his clients were.

As the interviewer responds, listen, listen, *listen* to determine how to customize your language. How does the interviewer frame each question?

"Do you think . . ." requires a logical, analytical answer.

"How do you see . . ." requires an innovative answer.

"How do you feel . . ." requires a compassionate answer.

"What's your sense . . ." requires an action-oriented answer.

None of these interpretations should surprise you; they are based on the information about personality types in Chapter 2.

Many positions require more than one interview; as you climb the interview ladder, remember who you're talking to. *Human resources* personnel screen candidates to match the job specification and recommend finalists. The *direct report* or *potential manager* evaluates your talent, intelligence, and personality. A *coworker* senses your compatibility and potential contribution, but also sees you as a possible competitor. When you're interviewing for a high-level position, the *management team* wants to see if you're the missing link to its success. Each interviewer has a different perspective that you must take into account.

If the position is high enough in the organization, you may be unlucky enough to be subjected to a "stress interview." This is a trial by fire during which the interviewer wants to strip you of your Sunday-best manners and find out how you *really* respond to pressure. Be on the lookout, because the stress interview often takes place in the most elegant of settings: dinner at a fine restaurant. It's easy to see why. As my father used to say, there are three ways to uncover a person's true character: get him drunk, play a competitive game, or lend him money. Thus, some executives will take you out to dinner, hoping that the atmosphere of conviviality will lead to drinking and the loosening of your tongue.

Accept a drink, but either sip it or don't drink it at all. There are ways to do this without appearing priggish. One good way to weaken the alcohol's potency is to wait for the ice cubes to melt. Or you might say you understand that the new Beaujolais has arrived and you'd love to taste it, but you're on antibiotics—could your dinner companions try it for you and tell you how it is? The idea is not to appear judgmental, just to sidestep the issue. Above all, don't confess that you're a teetotaler, even if you are. The Powers That Be want to test your sophistication and your ability to fit in—this is no time to establish yourself as the company Quaker. On the other hand, if the interviewer continues to sock down drinks, you may discover your potential boss is an alcoholic for whom you don't want to work.

Stay on your toes throughout the meeting and don't allow the interviewer to put you on the defensive, even if you feel there's something on your résumé that needs defending. For example, you might expect to be challenged over the fact that you've switched jobs frequently, or bounced from department to department in an effort to discover where you fit best. Explain that you're more valuable than the average candidate because you can see problems from several perspectives. There's a positive answer like this to every tough question.

Whoever your interviewer may be, and whatever office or restaurant you might find yourself in, try not to reveal your salary history, even during negotiations. If he asks how much money you want, it is wise to counter by asking what he's offering, or what your predecessor was paid. If the interviewer pressures you in the early stages, tell him you're showing your current employer the same courtesy you'll show at your new company—the courtesy not to discuss confidential matters while you are still employed. On the other hand, if you are approached by an executive recruiter who has certain specifications for a job he is trying to fill, you must give him your general salary range or total compensation package before he decides whether to introduce you to a prospective employer.

Large corporations often apply a plan such as the Hay Compensation Plan to guide them in deciding what to pay each worker. It's especially critical to negotiate aggressively if your dream job is at a company that utilizes one of these plans because your starting salary may determine your pay increases for years. Even at companies that don't follow a rigid compensation system like the Hay Plan, you must strategically pursue the highest possible salary up front. Someone who hops from company to company will often end up earning more than a person with similar skills who has spent his or her entire career at the same firm. In fact, the average career path includes nine or ten moves.

Unless it's your first job, always respond to a salary quote by asking for a few days to think it over. Among other things, this implies that you have another option. When you reply, ask charmingly if it's a final offer. The manager may up the ante if he's afraid of losing you. Don't accept an offer without knowing the entire package, including title, benefits, stock options, vacation, perks, off-site training, and travel and expense accounts. Inquire also about the company's expectations for your performance, your evaluation period, your operating budget, and your freedom to hire and fire. Get a letter of agreement before starting the job to verify the details agreed upon.

Throughout the final negotiation process, act confident and deserving of the position you've been offered. I once overheard an executive describe his latest coup—hiring a talented woman at a bargain-basement price. The candidate had painted a glowing picture of her track record, and a reference check substantiated her claims, but at the end of her interview, just as the interviewer was about to make a high-end offer, the woman unexpectedly interjected a submissive note of gratitude. This dampened the interviewer's enthusiasm and he gambled by making a low-ball bid, which the candidate accepted. A seller should never underestimate a buyer's willingness to pay dearly for something of value.

After a rewarding interview, it's considerate to thank the interviewer with a note, preferably mailed within twenty-four hours of the interview. Years ago thank-you notes were considered common courtesy; nowadays so few people observe this custom that sending one might actually nudge your name closer to the top of the list. If you type your note, use Monarch-size paper, 7 $\frac{1}{4}''$ × 10 $\frac{1}{2}''$, with the name, title, and address of your interviewer four lines below your signature rather than above the body of the letter. Why? The person you're writing to knows his own address; it's there for your benefit, not his. Putting it at the top detracts from the impact of the message itself. Witness this letter sent by George Bush during his term in office.

Notice that President Bush puts a line through "Mr. Fisher" and writes "Zach" in its place. The personal touch can influence the letter's reception in more ways than one; a secretary is more likely to give priority to a hand-addressed envelope than one with a computer-generated label that looks as if it could be part of a mass mailing.

If you write your thank-you note by hand, use a 4 $\frac{1}{2}''$ × 6 $\frac{1}{4}''$ correspondence card with your name engraved or printed at the top—no fancy monograms. It's thoughtful to show the same courtesy to the person who arranged the interview.

THE WHITE HOUSE

WASHINGTON

June 9, 1989

Dear Mr. *Zach* Fisher,

I am delighted to congratulate you on receiving the
Defense Distinguished Public Service Award. Few
individuals could be more deserving of this great
honor. Our entire Nation has been blessed by your
generous support of America's service men and women
and their families.

You have served your country quietly, with little
fanfare or acclaim, yet your contributions have
been outstanding. Since the end of World War II,
you've initiated and supported many wonderful
programs and activities that have helped to further
education, citizenship, and love of country in the
United States.

As a veteran, and now as Commander in Chief of
America's Armed Forces, I know how much your
generosity has meant to our Nation's military
community. It is a pleasure to join with your
friends, family and many admirers in saluting you.

Barbara joins me in sending you and Elizabeth our
warm best wishes.

Sincerely,

Mr. Zachary Fisher
42nd FLoor
299 Park Avenue
New York, New York 10017

HANDWRITING ANALYSIS

Once your résumé is polished to perfection, it's worth preparing for another aspect of the interview process: handwriting analysis. International companies, especially those in Western Europe, have long depended upon graphology as a reliable screening tool. Now the use of this technique.has become a fairly common practice among American companies as well. Your knee-jerk reaction to the topic of handwriting analysis might be: "I don't believe in it, so why pay attention to it?" I'll address the question of the validity of handwriting analysis later, but the more important point is that it really doesn't matter whether you believe in it or not. The companies you want to work for may believe in it.

Even if this is the first time you've heard that handwriting analysis is widely used to screen job candidates and decide who should move up the ladder, it's not a recent phenomenon. For years, select employers and recruiters have compelled job seekers to give them handwriting samples, often without their knowledge. It's possible you may have received a job offer—or lost one—partly because of a handwriting sample you didn't even realize you had produced.

Don't assume you're exempt if you're looking for an entry- or low-level job. The chief executive officer of a packaged goods company enlisted me recently to help him choose among seven possible applicants who sought to become his administrative assistant. This was a Jack- or Jill-Friday position that included handling correspondence, planning his business trips, and keeping his calendar. The CEO was especially concerned about the applicants' ability to handle pressure and keep his business affairs confidential.

I asked the candidates to allow me to submit their handwriting for analysis, promising that I would not ask the graphologist to delve into their childhoods. Each candidate accepted, and supplied me with a writing sample. Before the analysis, the CEO had narrowed the group down to two people. He was leaning toward Candidate A, the most sophisticated and well-spoken of the bunch. His second choice, Candidate B, seemed very bright but had an unpleasant voice and less appropriate hairstyle and clothing. The handwriting analysis told a different story.

Candidate A's Handwriting Analysis

"A has a strong need for security and attention. She wants recognition for herself and doesn't give a darn what it takes to get it or what other folks think about her. When it comes to pride, she has her own benchmarks.

"Her personal appearance is important and she is more kinesthetic than abstract. As a linear thinker, A wants to be efficient at her work so she makes lists and tries to organize her duties. If you tell her what is expected, you must give her plenty of room to operate in. She rankles at close authority and will grumble and complain when things don't go well. One weakness is her tendency to be a delayer."

Candidate B's Handwriting Analysis

"B is a very tactful person who understands the need to be diplomatic. When faced with a difficult situation, she instinctively knows how to sidestep unpleasantness. People will appreciate her fluid communicating style because she doesn't belabor a point. Those unable to keep up with her may find her too quick or too vague at times.

"One of her assets is the ability to change direction with ease. This is probably because she is highly intuitive and a quick study. She has a good sense of timing.

"B is a good starter who tends to dive right into her work. Some people need a detailed map of where they are to go and what they are to do. Not B—she can learn on her feet and find shortcuts to accomplish her goals.

"Although she enjoys responsibility, her ego needs are modest. She is basically shy and very sensitive. Personal privacy is important to B, so allow her a sense of distance and don't expect her to get involved in team efforts. She is more introspective than extroverted.

"When B is pushed, she will become evasive because she is sensitive. She operates in a more productive manner when asked rather than told to do something. B has a keen intelligence and things come naturally."

I don't need to tell you that the CEO took my advice and hired candidate B after seeing her handwriting analysis. Her positive report helped us see beyond the three-second impression her appearance and voice had made. I continued to work with her until she began to come across as the able self-starter her handwriting had shown her to be. Now at the company for several months, B has proved to be everything the evaluation promised.

During the screening process, especially at the initial interview that is sometimes conducted by a company's human resources department, job hunters are asked to fill out a form by hand—say, seven reasons why they want to join the firm. Often the questionnaire is a ruse to obtain the handwriting sample, which is sent to a handwriting expert who uses it to generate a psychological profile. Or the questionnaire serves two purposes, as the answers and handwriting are separately scrutinized. Certainly, no job is won or lost solely on the basis of a handwriting analysis, but it can play an important role in matching the right person to the right job.

How do you handle this situation tactfully? You can't compromise your job search by refusing to produce a handwriting sample, and you wouldn't want to spend weeks trying to copy the penmanship of some upstanding citizen such as Jackie Onassis or your Uncle Henry. Instead, on page 139 I'll describe some handwriting characteristics that indicate personality extremes so that you can eliminate them from your repertoire, even if only temporarily. For example, if you tend to fill up the page with words—a trait that's associated with invasiveness—it's easy to remember to leave margins on either side as you fill out forms during an interview. Remember, the whole point of modifying your approach to make a desirable impression is to show people what *you* want them to see.

Since successful corporations aren't usually susceptible to astrology-type voodoo, you might think twice about pooh-poohing the accuracy of graphology. In fact, you may already give it more credence than you realize. Have you ever seen a person's handwriting and drawn conclusions about him or her? Have you taken note of a person's handwriting that struck you as particularly artistic, or smiled at the unusual quirks of a charismatic friend's penmanship? Then you *do* believe, at least on some level, that handwriting says something about personality.

The theory behind handwriting analysis is that it's another form of body language—an unconscious expression of signals sent from the brain to the nerves that control the muscles in your hand. The hand, then, is the tool of the brain. Every aspect of slant, pressure, symmetry, and stroke reveal information about the writer's character. Surprisingly, neatness doesn't count, and a graphologist usually can't tell the age, gender, or nationality of the writer. What properly trained graphologists *can* diagnose, however, is astonishingly comprehensive: strengths, weaknesses, aptitudes, fears, integrity. They generally use many of the following traits to compose an evaluation:

Handwriting Analysis Criteria

Intelligence and judgment
   Comprehension, intuition, sensory perception, astuteness, judgment
Motivation
   Ambition, status, affluence
Competitiveness
   Dominating tendencies, aggressiveness, confidence
Communication skills
   Fluency, clarity verbally and written, diplomacy
Interpersonal relationships
   Temperament, composure, extroversive, introversive, leadership qualities—executive, supervisory, team leader or team player, empathy—harmonious or competitive, intellectual or emotional
Maturity and business aptitude
   Initiative, resourcefulness, reliability, perseverance, emotional stability, flexibility, self-esteem, risk-taking, integrity

Imagine: once you've handed in a writing sample, a potential employer who endorses graphology thinks he knows to what degree you possess the traits listed above. Some analysts' reports go so far as to tell what sort of relationship you had with your parents, or whether you'd ever be tempted to embezzle. It's the total impact of the writing on the page rather than the look of any one symbol or character that supplies this kind of information, but there are certain aspects of all handwriting that analysts agree are associated with negative traits. Avoid these if you want that job offer.

Patricia Peterson, the well-respected handwriting analyst, supplied the following signs for your consideration:

Positive Handwriting Traits

- A signature that goes slightly uphill, possibly with an underscore, indicates confidence.
- Clear and legible handwriting indicates a clear thinker.
- Adequate pressure on the pen demonstrates stamina and vitality.
- Desirable aesthetics include balanced margins and a straight baseline. Even if the writing flows uphill, you must be able to draw a straight line under the characters.
- Vigorous t-bars, with the crossbar drawn very high on the *t,* possibly rising at the end, indicates leadership and motivation.
- Diminutive writing indicates attention to detail.
- Large writing indicates entrepreneurial tendencies—a global thinker with a big ego.
- Simplification of letters without loss of legibility indicates a high IQ and maturity.

Negative Handwriting Traits

- An illegible scrawl with inconsistent style indicates a shady character or unbalanced personality.
- A light, feathery touch with the pen indicates a low energy level.
- Cramped writing indicates repression.
- Exaggerations of any type are unfavorable.

- A left-leaning slant made by a right-hander indicates fear and distrust.
- Lines that slant downward indicate pessimism.
- A cross-stroke near the top of a lower-case *t* may indicate an overbearing personality.
- Loops at the top of cursive *a*'s or *o*'s are a sign of insincerity.
- A signature that deviates little from the form in penmanship books indicates immaturity.
- An applicant who prints his work rather than using cursive writing may be hiding something, even if it's just the fact that his script is illegible!
- Flourishes or gigantic capitals indicate self-indulgence.

Changing your handwriting can backfire, of course; if you forget to make the change consistently throughout the document you may seem unstable. It might be worth investing $50 to $200 in a proper analysis of your own writing to find out what a company's graphologist will see. (Properly trained graphologists will produce nearly identical interpretations of the same writing sample.)

If your interviewer asks you to write something, and your intuition tells you it's for a handwriting analysis, courteously ask if it's for that purpose. If so, ask to see the results. The same applies to personality tests and proficiency exams used to determine your intelligence or suitability for a management position. Unfortunately, an interviewer will seldom share the results with you.

TARGETING A COMPANY

Interviewing for a job is like going on a blind date. While getting ready for the date many of us ask ourselves: "Will this person like me? Will this person want to see me again?" This is the wrong attitude. When preparing for an interview—or a blind date—we should spend just as much energy asking ourselves whether *we* will like the person we're meeting. During a job interview you should divide your efforts between pulling out all the stops to impress the interviewer and evaluating whether this position is one in which you'd be happy. This will keep you focused.

You're not likely to stay long in a job you hate, and such a mistake wastes your time *and* the company's. Better to determine whether the position is a good fit *before* committing all your resources to winning over the interviewer.

To prepare for negotiations, survey other companies to find out what they're paying people with comparable jobs. This isn't as tough as it sounds; just plug into the Internet or visit your local library and start hunting for articles in publications such as *Crains* that follow compensation. The information you find will help you judge how far to push your interviewer when he begins talking salary. I know of one job seeker who breached the company's computer network to find out the top salary for the job she wanted—although, of course, I don't recommend or endorse using such illegal tactics.

Ask friends and business contacts who may know about the job's responsibilities for their insights. If you're fuzzy on the details of the position, how can you decide whether it's right for you or explain to an interviewer why you fit the bill? Find out who your boss will be, as well as some details about his or her personality. Successful relationships depend on the right chemistry, so you don't want to leave it to chance. Ask how divisions are organized and how decisions are made. Is this an organization that meets your standards and can appreciate your contributions? Is this assignment complementary to your work style? Do you like to lead or follow? Do you prefer to work in groups or alone?

Once you've ascertained that this is a job in which you might be happy, study the company. As many times as job seekers have heard this advice, few actually heed it. Take advantage of a library's resources to bone up on the company's history, market standing, news coverage, and goals. Get to know the firm's product, whether it be diapers, bonds, or shoe polish. Read the firm's latest annual report and research trade association publications for articles about the company. As the manager who is hiring narrows his list of candidates, you can be sure that the most motivated one, the one who did his homework, has a good chance of making the best impression. A lot of work? Absolutely. In today's job market, it takes a lot of work to be the one who walks away with the offer.

But think of how much work you'll have saved if your favorite company hires you and you get to start a new job the next week instead of mailing out more résumés!

Before the interview, rehearse your pitch. Role-play with a friend or practice alone in front of a mirror. Can you cover all the pertinent information in ten minutes flat? Videotape a mock interview to remedy superfluous gestures and scowls. Record, then listen to yourself on a telephone answering machine to improve your voice, tone, diction, and speed. As I emphasized earlier, people with power speak slowly and clearly because they know they're important enough to be heard—and so are you.

THREE-SECOND OVERVIEW

All your ducks are in a row. You've learned how to market yourself for success with a résumé polished to perfection, and you can face the most challenging interview with confidence. In the next chapter, I'll take you inside the company with advice on how to perform with panache.

7

Presenting Yourself Inside the Company

OFFICE DECOR

Your haircut, your wardrobe, and your performance all came together to help you get the part—the job. From now on, your office is your stage. It can showcase your hard-won image or undermine it. Remember the walk I took down that law firm's hallways, telling the partner the personality traits of each office's occupant? Or Barry, the insurance exec who changed his office decor to confuse his superiors about his intentions? The look of your office or cubicle can actually help you rise in an organization.

The key is to be *orderly*. Many employees allow papers to pile up knee-high in their offices, trying to convey the impression they're overworked, understaffed, and intellectually superior. But these martyrs send the opposite message: that they're disorganized, sloppy, and undisciplined. For those who think their messy office makes them seem indispensable, I'll share the following story. I knew a man who was on vacation when his company announced a major restructuring. During his absence, his coworkers couldn't find anything they needed in his office. Rather than thinking him indispensable, his boss decided to dispense with *him* so that he could get a handle on the slob's projects.

Papers in an office should always be neatly arranged and properly filed, both on tabletops and in a desk. *Remember, your desk doesn't belong to you, nor does the work you generate—everything belongs to the company.* It follows that at least one other person on your staff should understand your filing system and be able to find key documents in your absence.

Imagine how you'd feel if a hurricane blew out the windows of your office and scattered its contents all over the street. Would you be embarrassed by what onlookers would find? Early in my career I prioritized the requests I gave to my secretary by marking them A, B, or C. Tasks to be completed that day were marked A, and lower-priority work was marked B or C. One night when I was working late I reached into my secretary's desk drawer to get a report I knew she kept there; instead, I found a pile of requests she'd hidden away when she fell behind. Apparently the secretary was more worried about saving face than she was about keeping up with her work. I hired a temp to help her catch up and all was resolved, but the point is that your office should be organized and free of personal papers or worrisome hidden evidence at all times. You never know when your well-crafted image will be destroyed by a manager working after hours who can't find what he's looking for (or who finds what he wasn't looking for).

The easiest ways to customize a standard office are to buy live plants and hang framed posters. Relegate faded photos to the circular file, keeping just a couple of framed pictures on your desk. Employees who work in cubicles need to be especially careful to keep personal effects to a minimum, reserving a drawer for their travel shoes or handbag to preserve their privacy.

As with so many other impression makers in business and social life, keeping a neat office is about looking like a decision maker, even if you aren't one yet. The higher you rise in a corporation—the more you use your brain—the fewer papers there are on your desk. CEOs' desks are whistle-clean. The obvious exceptions to this rule are lawyers, accountants, and other highly paid researchers or number crunchers. Back in the days when high society prevailed, notables had personal secretaries, maids, and other staff who kept things orderly. Now you'll have to do it yourself to convey the same impression of rank. If you take care of your work environment, your superiors are likely to conclude that you'll devote the same level of attention to your work.

SUPPORT STAFF

One of my clients spent thousands of dollars redecorating his company's offices in order to impress potential clients, then hired a gum-chewing receptionist to greet them. So much for his new, powerful image!

A receptionist or secretary delivers a first impression for you, whether over the telephone or at the door. Hiring a person with gracious manners sets the stage for your interactions with visitors both inside and outside the company. Don't tell me good help is hard to find—simply refocus your search. Oftentimes retirees, displaced execs, or the spouses of transferred managers are interested in such positions and have the courteous demeanor you seek.

An assistant should greet visitors or telephone callers by saying, "Good morning/afternoon, Mr./Ms. X." Even if it sounds too formal, the best approach in any business situation involving greetings is to start with the most formal address and work your way down from there. Titles are a measure of power, and a person's full name is his most basic title. When I come across a secretary with an informal attitude, who immediately calls me Camille, I can't allow the informality to stand; it sets a tone of disrespect that might infect my dealings with the secretary's boss. Here's how I rectify the faux pas and get the assistant on my side; try this method the next time someone neglects to address you properly.

"What is your full name?" I ask.

"Donald Smith."

"Oh, Mr. Smith, please tell Ms. Exec that Mrs. Lavington is calling. If she's not too busy I'd like a couple of minutes of her time."

If the person I'm speaking to is working in a formal organization, I move on. If, however, I'm speaking to someone in an informal organization, I approach it differently. When the assistant gets back on the line to tell me he's putting me through, I'll thank him and say, "Donald, I don't know you yet, but I hope when we meet you'll please call me Camille.'' The next time I speak to the assistant I'll tell him that Camille Lavington is on the line.

Hogtie your company's receptionist if you hear phrases like "Hold the phone, honey" or "He's on the other line, dearie." Oddly, it's female assistants who often fall into this trap, treating other women chauvinistically but speaking deferentially to men.

On your part, show as much consideration for receptionists as possible, both to ensure that you get what you need and to accord them the respect they deserve. They're the "keepers of the gate." Greet them cordially, give the full name of the person you'd like to speak to, and offer your own name, company, title, as well as the purpose of your call. Begin any request with the words "May I." If your call goes directly through to the person you were dialing, identify yourself and ask if it's a convenient time to speak for a few minutes. If the individual is on the other line, in a meeting, or concentrating on some important matter, you lose points if you resist his or her request to speak at another time. Offer to call back at a more convenient time, or leave your number.

Calls bounced to voice mail make clarity even more important. Pace your message at a slower rate than your usual speaking voice and recite your phone number slowly. If your phone call isn't returned within two business days, be an eagle—assume the message was lost or garbled. Call again with an upbeat tone.

These suggestions may seem obvious, but there are business people the world over being frustrated by the poor phone manners of others. How many times have you waited a week to return the phone call of someone whose business wasn't important to you? How can you be sure that this person will not be in a position to help you at some point in the future? Showing respect for everyone is the best way to protect their feelings and your reputation. Just because everyone else's standards are low doesn't mean yours have to be.

MEETINGS, MEETINGS, MEETINGS

Rule Number One: The meeting itself is never more important than the preplanning that goes into it.

Rule Number Two: There is always a hidden agenda, even in the most innocuous of gatherings.

The above rules may seem a bit paranoid, but I guarantee they are ironbound. The most harmless-sounding meeting I've heard about recently was one in which an organization asked some managers together to discuss the idea of taking a group photo of the employees, which would appear in company brochures for the upcoming year. The managers rubber-stamped the notion, and the photo was taken. It turned out that the head of the division had asked for the photo at holiday time because he was planning to fire a number of women at the beginning of the calendar year and wanted the mixed-sex photo to deflect attention from the company's sexist practices.

A meeting can be a briefing, a debriefing, or a test of power games. No one can divine the true purpose of every company assembly, but following certain guidelines can keep you out of the line of fire.

Holding a Meeting

Before you schedule a meeting, consider whether it's really necessary. Too many meetings can ruin a company—very few of them have anything to do with productivity. It's easy to limit them by speaking to people individually, handing out assignments, and leaving employees alone to work.

Once you've determined that you can't live without this particular get-together, invite no more than eight participants—that is, if you actually want to accomplish something. In a larger meeting, the forward movement is arrested by the splintering of the group into subsets of people who are pro, people who are con, and one rabble-rouser. Even in a room with fewer than nine people, there will usually be a bad apple, someone who wants negative attention. Sometimes you don't have to do anything to control this person— the group will feel drained by his insistence on jabbering about his favorite topic and will turn on him—but at other times you'll have to defuse him in order to pursue your own agenda.

One method for controlling bad apples is to send out a memo detailing the meeting's subject matter. When one person keeps derailing the meeting you can use the contents of the memo as an excuse to return to the topic at hand. Giving each participant a time limit for his presentation usually helps, as does telling someone that you'll discuss his concerns later in your office. I've arranged for negative types to be called out of meetings after a certain interval in order to limit the damage they can do. The point is not to humiliate them in public, but to blunt their negativism and allow them the opportunity to vent their spleen at a less disruptive time.

An executive I knew always planted an ally, whose purpose was to deflect attention from time-suckers. A signal from the exec would spur the ally to tell the troublemaker that he had a good point and to ask him to put it in writing and hand it in the next morning. The ally had thus made the person feel important—and, after all, sometimes the concerns of talkaholic employees are worth noting.

Predetermine your allies and gain support for your proposal by arranging friendly trade-offs before the meeting begins. Never, ever forget a favor owed, especially when it is easily repaid. When your proposal is accepted, spread the glory so that the other participants will be more inclined to make the project itself a success. When that day arrives, spread the glory some more.

If you're presenting a new idea, work your way into it. To quote Machiavelli: "It must be considered that there is nothing more difficult to carry out, nor more doubtful of success, nor more dangerous to handle, than to initiate a new order of things." Base the new concept on a successful tradition, no matter how far-fetched, to make it appear as if your innovation is simply a variation on the status quo. Toss out a couple of red herrings to be shot down before presenting your darling. If you need more time to win your point, call the current meeting a preliminary, fact-finding session. Later, call a second meeting and find some way to exclude the nay-sayers.

To emphasize the importance of a new order, hold the meeting off site, where there will be no distractions. Then limit the length of the gathering, using the clock to force decisions. No matter how heated or acrimonious the debate, conclude on a positive note—you may need some of these players later.

Don't assume you have to meet a potential client on her territory, where you may feel at a disadvantage. Invite her to a breakfast or luncheon at a private club or restaurant—breaking bread is a time-honored method of building rapport.

The length of the meeting and the identity of the participants should determine whether you serve refreshments. If decision-makers are invited, you must feed them first to break the ice and make them more receptive to your ideas. An internal meeting of an hour or longer requires soda and coffee so that the participants can keep up their blood sugar. Plus, having drinks together increases camaraderie and team spirit.

Secretaries and administrative personnel hate setting up drink bars and supplying pads and pencils for meetings because it makes them feel like waitresses, but these are the things that make meetings function. The same goes for checking equipment before the gathering and rustling up an extra extension cord—I've seen many a politically loaded meeting go awry because of the lack of essential supplies.

Participating in a Meeting

In advance of the meeting, write on a card three or four points you'd like to make or questions you'd like to have answered. Often, in the heat of the moment, people forget to establish resources, budgets, time frames, and responsibility. Then they're left holding the bag when something goes wrong.

Judicious timing is the key to success in a meeting. Withhold your comments until the participants have had a chance to mull over the advantages or disadvantages of the proposal before them. When you do put in your two cents, keep your remarks brief; it's best to be perceived as someone who has established a pattern of thoughtful responses. Before you shoot down an idea, consider how your just-being-honest impressions will be received—your observations may backfire the next time you're trying to persuade someone whose program you have openly opposed.

Holding your tongue can have another benefit: a speaker often doesn't reveal his agenda until the last three minutes of his presentation. This dynamic occurs most frequently at impromptu meetings when you're called into your boss's office. No matter how nervous you may be, sit back and wait for him to state his real intentions. The wrong comment made too early could produce a negative outcome.

Don't pretend a meeting is democratic if it's not. Our era of so-called "team management" has lulled many mid-level employees into letting down their guard during company conclaves. Remember that no matter how "flat" the hierarchy, the person with rank always pulls it once the meeting becomes controversial. Believe me, a superior may delay his response to what he perceives to be disloyalty; but, like an elephant, he does remember, and at some point he will retaliate.

Case Study: Dick, 47

Dick was the well-respected publisher of a medical trade magazine that had just been acquired by a major conglomerate. The conglomerate had never owned a publication in that field. Unfortunately, at his first meeting, Dick disagreed with his new boss in front of other people. Little did he realize the extent of the boss's ego until he found himself transferred to the boondocks six months later.

When my clients complain to me about the outcome of meetings they've attended, they're usually unhappy about not getting enough recognition for a contribution they've made. I tell them to get over it. Eagles know that it doesn't really matter who gets credit as long as the job gets done. Beating your chest and pulling your hair to get attention will just make you look like someone who doesn't see the big picture. Everyone knows that bosses steal their subordinates' thunder; but then, that's how companies are set up. The boss is the one who gives you the budget or resources to get the job done. Unorthodox as this may sound, he or she should take the credit. When you're the boss, you can do it too.

If, however, a colleague habitually takes credit for your work, you can use a meeting to provide witnesses for your ideas. The same goes for a sticky situation in which two associates try to play off one another to delay giving you an answer to a question or making a commitment to a project. Invite both of them to the meeting, force the issue, and they'll have lost the leverage they had when you were shuttling between them.

Whether you're the host or a guest at a meeting, here are some tips for successfully leaving your mark:

MEETING MASTERY
- Be the first or last one to enter the room.
- Sit facing the door, at the center of a long table.
- Avoid sitting in front of a window; light distracts.
- Never spring a surprise on a superior.
- Delay decisions if you're not winning.
- Make vague promises, such as cutting taxes after the election.

PREPARING A SPEECH

Before putting pen to paper or mouse to pad, analyze your audience. Consider what they know, what they need to know, and how to tell them what you want them to know. A good speech is delivered with style, but it begins with an objective that is clearly stated or implied. This is delivered via the title or an opening statement. The two most important moments of your delivery are the opening and the closing. Capture the audience's interest and end with a statement they can remember.

Your listeners need to acclimate themselves to your voice, so at the beginning of your speech make a timely or humorous remark. This is the crucial moment when you establish your bond with the audience. It affects their attitude toward the rest of your speech. Have a few good openers in your back pocket—ones you are familiar with so they come across in a natural way.

Remember, there are only two reasons anyone is listening to your speech: to be entertained or to be educated. Your title or opener indicates what they are about to hear. My advice is to cover no more than three or four main topics, with up to three subheadings behind each topic. Begin by drawing up an outline:

- *Objective*—determine the theme you want the audience to remember.
- *Title*—create a punchy or provocative title to draw interest and increase attendance.
- *Topics*—accommodate only three main concepts in a twenty-minute speech; that's all an audience can absorb.
- *Closing*—synthesize all the information into one final statement.

PUBLIC SPEAKING

The number one fear shared by 98% of people in business is the prospect of public speaking. *The Book of Lists* mentions that speaking before a group ranks first of the fourteen worst human fears. Death, by contrast, comes in sixth, with the natural conclusion that public speaking is a fate worse than death.

This includes not only speeches before the public but also company presentations to colleagues and executives, and company meetings.

Rather than succumb to this fear and kiss your prospects of recognition goodbye, take heed of this fail-safe technique. If you follow these guidelines, public speaking will become a pleasure. (Fear of anything comes from inexperience; the more often you do something, the easier it becomes.)

Know Your Material

Read the previous section on preparing a speech, especially noting the advice on targeting your audience. Then practice, practice, practice in front of a mirror or with a friend, or tape yourself on an audio or video recorder. Psych yourself up by getting so involved in your material that you forget about your own self-consciousness.

Calm Your Nerves

Just before stepping on stage, clench your hands together firmly in front of you, or squeeze the arms or seat edge of your chair, and hold your breath for five seconds. This simple exercise will engage your adrenal and give you a minute or so to relax before your speech without being paralyzed by stage fright.

Own the Room

Any great performer knows that he must walk onstage and fill the room with his presence. Following this simple set of directions to the letter, no matter how silly some may seem, you will hold any audience spellbound.

Organize your ''fan club.'' Imagine your four greatest supporters seated nearby—one front center, another two at each side exit, and your spouse at the rear. You may not be on stage, but this can work for you. The intimidating CEO sitting to your right appears a lot less fearsome. Prepare your own ''fan club'' for your next public speaking opportunity. Whenever I speak publicly I always imagine there are two or three people on stage who believe in me—these could be friends, family members, or colleagues.

Take Your Three Seconds

When you walk on, you have three seconds to establish your ground and capture the room. Here's how it works:

Take Three Deep, Relaxing Breaths. Do not miss this step, because it is the third breath that anchors you. While you're breathing, sweep the room with your eyes and smile at your audience, locating your ''fan club'' while you're at it. Make eye contact and get the measure of the crowd, taking them in with your breaths. As you're doing this, remember that the audience is taking their three seconds to bond with you. Remember that *they* need the time as much as you do. It may feel like an eternity, but these three seconds will establish your presence, power, and command over the group.

Warm Up the Audience. Say something light, off the cuff, a joke or a word of welcome or praise about the audience, the town, the company. It should be the most well-rehearsed phrase in your speech. This gives your audience a chance to get to know your voice, defuses the tension, and completes the bond before you start on your material. At this point, your three seconds are up.

Barbara Browning, the respected media coach who prepares authors for television and public speaking, suggests three ways to be certain that people will listen when you speak.

Look at Your Audience. Eye contact helps to keep your listeners alert and interested in your message. It also enables you to gauge your effectiveness by seeing their reactions.

Can Every Word Be Understood? Articulate with energy; it shows your commitment to your subject. Avoid Using "Uhs" and "You knows." Replace them with pauses. Don't be afraid of silence. We are not necessarily thinking when we say, "uh" or "you know," we are just filling in space. Use a pause instead, and what you say will sound more thoughtful.

Be Posture Perfect. Stand tall, sit tall, and keep your head level, not tilted to the side. Body weight should be evenly distributed over both feet when you stand to address a group. You will look better and sound better.

Do not leave an audience's reaction to chance. Not only can you gauge the audience response, you must do so continually throughout the event, adjusting your style until you and your listeners have bonded, and they have embraced your ideas. Only then will you know your words have had the impact you intended.

When giving a presentation—it doesn't matter whether you're pitching an ad campaign to a company or a fund-raising strategy to a charity—in order for your speech to be successful, you must lead the audience through a decision-making process that ends with their endorsement of your plan. The structure of the interaction between audience and speaker should proceed as follows—the terms apply whether you adopt the speaker's point of view or the audience's, as I'll demonstrate later on:

Listen. The purpose of the beginning of the talk is to grab the audience's attention. Just because they're sitting there doesn't mean they're devoting any energy to listening, which is a very active process. Most effective speakers start off with a joke because the audience needs a transition from focusing on their own thoughts to focusing on your words. Humor works best; as I keep repeating, people generally want to be entertained before being educated.

This transition device of humor also helps the audience to adjust to your pace, tone, and voice. These should be pleasing to the ear, just as your appearance should be pleasing to the eye and present an image the audience can relate to. Then, like a good preacher, repeat your main point three times to make sure the audience gets it, working it into the lecture from different angles to sound fresh.

Assess. Some people have a way of listening but not really paying attention; of hearing but not digesting the information before them. It's easy to assess their attentiveness by observing their body language. Any expression can indicate attention—from alert to puzzled to irritated. That means they're deciding for themselves whether your viewpoint is one they should consider. Slack jaws, staring into space, or doodling on a pad means they're ever so subtly booing you off the stage. Time to change course!

Bridge. Build rapport by sharing information the audience would consider especially engaging, given their point of view. Your listeners will then further scrutinize the information by applying their own standards of reasoning.

Adapt. Change course midstream if your approach isn't having the desired effect. Do more of whatever has gone over well and jettison any angle that gets no response. Allow for this eventuality in the preparation of your presentation. Know your material!

Acknowledge. This step is especially obvious at a meeting, where the discussion opens up for commentary and decision-making. As the audience examines the angles, it becomes clear whether the speaker is being affirmed. The speaker should take pains to give credit or praise the audience's field of interest.

Empower. The speaker suggests ways for members of the audience to improve their performance.

Endorse. On the part of the audience, this step often occurs out of earshot of the speaker. The attendees walk out the door, discussing possible outcomes of an idea they clearly sanction. Endorsement on the part of the speaker involves a reinforcing statement of praise for the audience and its industry.

To further illustrate these concepts, let's apply them to an example in which you're pitching a fund-raising strategy to a philanthropic organization. Now we're looking at this process from the point of view of a member of the audience rather than that of the speaker. A board member first *listens* to the new strategy. He then *assesses* whether the plan will preserve the dignity of the cause while attracting enough dollars to finance the next year's activities. The board member thinks about previous fund-raising drives and wonders whether the new campaign will be a *bridge* from the previous one; will the continuity of the charity's image be broken by departing from what worked in the past? He then recognizes how to *adapt* one aspect of the fund drive to make it fly (you've got him here!). As he discusses his ideas with the presenter, he *acknowledges* the merits of the strategy. Satisfied that the changes he's requested will be made, he *empowers* the presenter by outlining the resources he'll devote to the effort. After the presentation has ended, he puts his political power behind the new fund-raising drive to demonstrate his *endorsement.*

NEGOTIATE SO EVERYONE WINS: POWER SECRET #8

All negotiating flows from the same principle: pretend you're playing poker, and never reveal your strategy; know when to raise the ante, go eye to eye, call the other person's bluff, back off, and bluff, bluff, bluff.

Whatever carrot you're chasing, it's best to make your request when the boss is most receptive to it. Make an appointment early in the week, but not on Monday because we all need a day to get back into the groove of the work week. Take care also to make the appointment early in the day—over breakfast if possible—to avoid ringing phones and other distractions. Never ask for anything after lunch from people who've had a few drinks. They're never magnanimous then.

What if the person you need to meet with is too tough to corner? Be creative, but don't sacrifice your dignity. One client of mine was gunning for a transfer to a department whose boss was always traveling on business. I instructed her to smile and jokingly say: "Your schedule seems so busy, why don't I meet you in the parking lot with a cup of coffee when you return from your next trip?'' You can suggest a brief meeting as you ride in the elevator together on the way to a lunch meeting, or talk while you pump iron at the company's fitness club. One employee who wanted to save her skin during a messy takeover asked her chairman for twenty-three minutes—one minute for each year she had worked at the company.

Build relationships with administrative assistants or human resources staffers who will alert you when changes are afoot. A secretary who has just typed up a memo from her boss about the division's quarterly loss can warn you not to ask for a raise until the sun comes out. Knowing someone who can advise you about the ideal time to ask for a raise, transfer, or promotion can ensure a successful result.

To radically increase your raise or bonus as Barry did in Chapter 1, find out the review schedule and begin your campaign three months before the big day. Senior management needs to think that your goal was their idea. Prior to this promotion period, take every opportunity to put some kind of good news or progress report on the manager's desk, describing not just your accomplishments but their effect on the bottom line. Making your supervisor aware of your good deeds supplies him with the evidence he'll need to defend your increase to the powers *he* has to answer to.

One month before review time, approach your boss and tell him that you know he'll have to write a report about your performance soon, so you've prepared some performance figures to demonstrate your progress over the past year. If you've made mistakes, show how you've corrected the situation without sounding defensive. Use psychodynamics to present this information in a way that will harmonize with the supervisor's style. If he's a thinker, wait until you have concrete facts to offer. If he's a feeler, work to turn his emotions around.

A woman from a television network came to me protesting that she was powerless to renegotiate her contract; it was written each year by a squad of lawyers. Fine, I said, start negotiating next year's contract the day after you sign this year's. Find out what they're paying your competitors and put your division head on notice that you won't allow yourself to be railroaded anymore. She wasn't.

To prepare for the Big Day, envision that you're seated at the negotiating table. Keep silent. Listen to what your supervisor is proposing, and tell him you'd like to think about it overnight. You don't have to accept his offer. The person who's giving the evaluation most likely has more in his back pocket than he brings out, especially if you're at the height of your career. My favorite line is: "I'd like to consider your proposal. Would you do me a favor and sharpen your pencil? Let's talk tomorrow."

When you return to the negotiating table, wait to see how sharp the manager's pencil is. If it appears that no more money is forthcoming, ask for more benefits, perks like a car allowance, the initiation fee at a private club, a larger travel and expense account, or a smashing new title that will look impressive to the outside world. Executives of high enough standing can request an equity position in the company.

Stubborn manager? Counter his attitude by saying: "I realize that the morale of the department, strong sales growth, and retaining good staff are all important objectives (substitute whatever applies to you). I can accomplish those things when I feel good about my compensation here, which will make you look good and cause your compensation to rise as well." You haven't implied that you'll jump ship—doing so would only irritate him. But, by referring to the notion that team members quit when morale is low, you'll have given him the hint without ever having to make a threat.

As you negotiate, keep in mind a figure below which you will not go. Your spies in human resources or in the typing pool should be able to tell you what the average raise is; if your manager insists on a below-average figure, you've been given fair warning that he or she may not keep you around for long. It may settle your mind to bring the issue right out into the open. Ask: "What is your long-term plan for me? I can be patient as long as I know there's a pot of gold at the end of the rainbow." If the executive indicates that your future is cloudy, tell him that you appreciate his candor and will give him your best while you're there. Then walk out the door and send out your résumé.

Early in my career, one of my managers named a figure for my upcoming raise. I repeated the number three times quizzically, and he countered with a higher offer. You can try this even if you're satisfied with the amount—the negotiator will increase the sum if he's feeling guilty about his initial quote.

During uncertain periods, such as when a company is considering a merger, tactics such as these may be too aggressive. After all, companies in play are looking to dump staff, and you don't want to end up at the top of the list. In these circumstances, the best you can do is to ask for some protection. Suggest that you'll accept the salary if you can have a six- or eight-month guarantee, at which time you'll have another review. Once you're in a company, you can't request a golden handshake, but a silver one might buy all the time you need.

Say you've taken a job and found that it's not what it was represented to be. Your bonus might not have been what you were led to expect, or the work situation might not agree with you. Whatever the reason, it won't affect your career if you choose not to stick with it. I often hear employees in untenable situations say that they can't leave a job they've held for less than six months or a year. Why not? Leave it off your résumé. If an interviewer asks about the interruption in your work history, remember that many factors can keep people from working continuously through their adult lives. Tell the interviewer you've been taking care of family business or involving yourself in family property management. If the interviewer probes further, tell him politely that you'd rather not discuss it. He or she can assume that you've been managing family investments or caring for a sick parent. Plus, answers like these reinforce the walk-away attitude we all must cultivate in negotiations.

PERFORMING WITH FINESSE

Just as there are people who seem able to eat anything they like without gaining weight, there are workers in every office who seem to get what they want without ever sullying their reputations. These people have finesse, and you can have it too if you know their secrets.

Kiss the Babies

This symbolic expression is priceless; I touched on it in Chapter 1. Many people learned in school that "brown-nosing" is a sin, so they go overboard trying to maintain distance. I think that currying favor has gotten a bad rap. How else do you get people on your side? In fact, *not* cultivating good will can have a chilling effect on your career. If you forgo certain courtesies or hesitate to repay them, you'll be vulnerable to manipulation by adversaries waiting to retaliate at some unexpected moment in the future. Acknowledge people at every level, from clients to subordinates to superiors—after all, the boss is a baby too.

The number one issue for nearly every worker is recognition, not salary. Praise is a powerful motivator. Kissing the babies can create a congenial working atmosphere that inspires employees to perform, making you—their manager—look especially good. Combine praise with an understanding of psychodynamics and you can save your department a lot of money. Why? Listen hard to the way a discontented employee voices his complaint. He may be asking for higher pay, but more challenging assignments and a greater degree of acknowledgment are what would really satisfy him.

Even criticism can go down more smoothly if it's covered in sugar. I tell clients to make criticism the filling in a sandwich of praise. Begin with a compliment, follow with a critique, and then end on a positive note, acknowledging the employee's contributions. When I speak to groups of executives, I often shock them by saying, "Bless your hearts, you try so hard, but you're a mess." The gentle tone at the beginning of the sentence softens them up while the punch line takes them off guard. They're often more receptive to my message after I've set up my program this way.

"Bless your heart, you're a mess" also demonstrates how much humor can influence the outcome of an interaction. Tickle someone's funny bone and he'll withhold his judgments a little longer. That doesn't apply to meanspirited teasing; however, I've noticed that, when people are thrown into predicaments beyond their capabilities, they demean those who have a higher standard. But kidding someone who insists on quality or who has made a mistake inevitably lowers morale.

Be Patient

It takes nine months to make a baby, yes? Nothing worth having comes quickly or easily. It takes three visits to influence a decision maker and a year to change your destiny. You must allow time for the person you're trying to impress to adjust his point of view. It requires a great investment of time and energy to flatter the decision maker, empower him with the ability and responsibility to help you achieve your goals, and place yourself under his protection. Few people who are given the power to change someone's life will deny themselves the satisfaction of wielding that power.

Distance Yourself from Negative Information

As I discussed in Chapter 5, sophisticated people speak indirectly. Sophisticated employees also *operate* indirectly. They let others carry the sword and don't get blood on their hands. If there are unpopular changes to be made in a department, they give the responsibility for achieving those goals to a subordinate who takes the heat. Although people in the department may suspect that you are the one behind the changes, you have not implicated yourself. A sophisticated executive always lets someone else swat the mosquitoes.

Eagles delegate the job of putting employees on notice without incurring their wrath. They explain that a directive has come from above. Employees who are being released are told that the "Big Boss" has said the numbers don't add up so the division is being downsized.

There's a flip side to knowing that no one in business can ever be trusted to keep a secret. Eagles use deliberate gossip to disseminate information they don't want connected to them. Think of Deep Throat during the Watergate scandal. He leaked information and achieved his objectives, yet to this day none of us knows his identity. I don't want my clients to be ugly, but I want them to be effective and protect themselves at the same time.

Handle the Press Graciously

The job interview isn't the only time you'll be forced to answer difficult questions; throughout your work life you may be confronted with press conferences or journalists calling for quotes. Before consenting to be interviewed, consult your company's public relations department and ask for their guidance. If you're on your own, consider whether accepting an interview request from a publication outside your industry—however prestigious—is worth your time. Many executives allow themselves to be dazzled by the name of the publication and later regret devoting their energies to an outlet that can't possibly help their careers. Oftentimes the only person they've helped by going on record is the writer.

Speak carefully—thinking out loud is the easiest way to get quoted in a way that puts you in a bad light. The same can be said for speaking off the record; while many journalists keep confidences, you can never be sure how well your identity will be protected.

Disregard the spin the reporter puts on the article he's researching and try to divine his agenda for yourself. Make yourself a valued source by volunteering to supply information not just about yourself and your company but about the industry as a whole. If a reporter thinks he will need you for other stories down the road, he's more likely to portray you favorably this time around.

Send a thank-you note to the reporter when your conversations are concluded. If you're heavily quoted or if the story is a profile of you, take the journalist to lunch or give him a small gift to show your appreciation when the issue hits the newsstands. Building rapport with writers can save you thousands of public relations dollars.

Follow Through

Living up to a reasonable promise is far more important than making an extravagant one. If you doubt you can keep your word, don't give it in the first place, or at least make it clear that you will do your absolute best but cannot promise results. When you agree to handle a project, drop your boss a brief note to mark its completion. Respond to every request for information within hours, not days.

Favors aren't to be given, they're to be traded. Following through is vital when someone does you a favor. If you take advantage of someone without a sense of obligation, you're asking for trouble later. Reinforce your peers' view of your graciousness by returning favors both openly and behind their backs. At every opportunity, praise the person who has treated you well, even if word won't necessarily get back to him or her. Eagles know there's no free lunch.

Engage in Reciprocity

Exchanging favors is one of the most effective ways to finesse your way to success. Balance is everything. Do favors for others, even without being asked, to establish a relationship in which each party looks out for the other's interests. Return favors quickly and appropriately—one who ignores obligations is soon *persona non grata!*

A top executive with an international trade firm in Britain asked me to handle several tasks. When he decided to change jobs, he hired me to assist in his search. I moved mountains to help him, and he ultimately became head of a prominent company in Canada.

Later I was asked to address a convention in his city, and he invited me to have dinner at some point during my visit. The morning before my speech, I chipped a tooth and sought his help. He never returned my call. Quite recently he flew into New York to seek another job and called for my assistance and contacts. You can guess my reaction. I personally believe there is an unwritten obligation to repay people for favors.

The offending client in the preceding story was a man, but in my experience it's my female clients who need lessons in reciprocity. Men seem to take it for granted that trading favors is an unspoken rule of conducting business. Women, by contrast, seem to view favors as social obligations that don't extend to business. It's unfortunate, because every time a woman overlooks an opportunity to do a favor or return a favor, she's broken the chain she's building.

THREE-SECOND OVERVIEW

You've learned new ways to handle people with finesse, give an interesting speech, and negotiate successfully. In the next chapter, you'll find out about the skulduggery that goes on behind the scenes—nearly everywhere!

8

Behind Closed Doors at the Office

There are three levels of interaction in every workplace: what everyone sees, what some people see, and what no one but the boss sees. All the workers in an office might observe the hustle and bustle as they scramble to meet an important deadline. Only the managers, however, know that their employees' performance on the project will determine which ones will be allowed to keep their jobs after an upcoming merger. Even managers don't realize that the division head has searched all their offices during the night to make sure they were telling the truth about their progress toward the department's goal. The dirty tricks that happen behind closed doors make a knowledge of psychodynamics crucial.

USE YOUR INSTINCTS: POWER SECRET #9

Many of us are naive about what really goes on behind the scenes at work, partly because we need to trust people and feel secure in our working environment. The very thought of watching our backs every moment would drive us mad. I understand this need but, after spending twenty years in the corporate world, I've concluded that having too much confidence in an employer's maturity and respect for your privacy is a recipe for disaster. You'll be shocked at some of the stories I tell in this chapter, but I urge you not to assume that the misdeeds I describe aren't happening at your office. They probably are—you just don't know about them. Presume that any or all of them are taking place at this very moment and protect yourself. You're not being paranoid, just cautious and circumspect.

OFFICE LAND MINES

Late-Night Searches

This is one of the most common dirty tricks bosses play, and the one my clients are slowest to believe is happening to them. "You don't know my boss," they tell me. "He would never go hunting in my desk." Yet some of the most benevolent, mild-mannered executives make a regular practice of going through their subordinates' files. For example, a famous mogul made clandestine weekend rounds at his Manhattan headquarters on a monthly basis to sniff out his employees' secrets. He checked to see if they were making their quotas, reading romance novels on company time, or mailing out résumés.

The executive ferreted out the slackers, substance abusers, and slobs who left spoiled food in their desks. He then took great pleasure in tormenting these people to see if they would admit to their bad acts or lack of performance. He'd ask them how they were progressing with an important client or on a key report, and then watch them squirm. If the exec wasn't overly eager to keep someone at the company, he'd call them on their deceptions. They were always stunned by what he knew, but none jumped to the conclusion that he'd taken a stroll through their personal papers. Instead they assumed he was clairvoyant.

As I discussed in Chapter 6, treat your office space like a garage. You can park there for the day, but you don't own the space. It belongs to the company, and the company provides you with the materials you need to complete your work. That work, plus the space you accomplished it in and the resources you used, all belong to the company. They have the right to poke around at any time, and not just to sniff out wrongdoing. Many a worker has gotten the ax after a superior found something unexpected when innocently looking for a report he legitimately needed.

Good Old Boys

Whenever men congregate away from the office, they brag openly about their latest conquests and challenges. We used to refer to it as the Good Ole Boys' Club, because it was always held outside the buttoned-up business environment. But whether in the locker room, on the golf course, or at a club, men share information that eventually *leaks back* to the boss. It's also a major communications pipeline that excludes women, and many men prefer it that way. They intentionally share this information in same-sex surroundings in order to maintain an advantage over their female colleagues—after all, women talk the same way among themselves. It's a dirty trick because women generally aren't privy to confidential information, so the battle stories they exchange don't help them to advance. Senior men pass down their methods for landing a tough account or making a political move to junior male employees, and the cycle continues.

As an aside, women who conduct business overseas should know that this attitude—that females are second-class citizens—is much more institutionalized abroad than it is in the United States. Railing at the gods won't change things—only the artful practice of psychodynamics will force businessmen to recognize the contributions of their female associates.

If you are an ambitious professional, you should resist the impulse to *react emotionally* when you find yourself in a one-down position at work. Playing the role of martyr won't prompt any senior executive to change his viewpoint. If you discover you're actually being excluded from meetings, come right out and ask to be included. If you can't attend, talk to a friend who did, or, if minutes were taken, ask to read them afterward.

Many professional groups are single-gender-oriented; if you're in one, consider bypassing the group in favor of industry associations where information flows across both sides of the gender fence.

I tell my female clients that they should make an effort to identify themselves as business people, not business women. Success lies in accepting the fact that the world won't change overnight; if it's still a man's world, play the game the way the men do rather than insisting on a stereotypical feminine style that isn't getting you anywhere. You're relationship-oriented, whereas they are transaction-oriented. They like to win and will battle for victory, but afterward they don't personalize the outcome. Women tend to hold grudges; instead, follow the men's lead by duking it out and walking away. Build your constituency and find subtle ways of claiming credit for your accomplishments. Use your knowledge of personality types to adjust your presentation to suit any audience.

As for the next generation of career women, give your daughter lessons in games like tennis, soccer, karate, chess, backgammon, or bridge at an early age so she'll become a convivial competitor and a strategic thinker. Perhaps one day women's empathetic way of doing business will become the norm, but if it doesn't, she'll be prepared to go head to head with the best of the boys.

Beware of the Spouse

Sad to say, your spouse can tank your career. When I have a significant assignment to polish an individual who is about to take on increased responsibility or meet a CEO for an important interview, I always request that the couple meet me for dinner before they face an evening with the mogul in charge.

Part of the reason is that the spouse may need the same kind of polishing as the client, but the other part is that the spouse can undo much of what I help my clients to accomplish. Because the partner doesn't see the big picture, he or she can counter my influence by pressuring my client to reject my advice.

The most dangerous spouses are those who are both ambitious and naive. Lacking in social skills, these spouses have a way of opening their mouths and scuttling a contract. Corporations are aware of this problem, which is one reason they no longer open up business events to significant others. In the fifties and earlier, male business executives' wives played a major part in their husbands' advancement, entertaining clients and bosses at home. Now that successful business people come from more diverse backgrounds, their spouses have varying degrees of sophistication, and companies have learned that involving them is just as likely to scotch a deal as to seal it.

One of my clients, whom I'll call Louis, worked for a biotechnology corporation that merged with a French multinational organization. He was asked to go to Paris to meet the principals, and his company hired me to coach him on his social graces and protocol. I found Louis to be smart and tough, but lacking in social skills.

At the last minute, Louis's wife, Doris, was invited to join him on the trip. I offered to coach her too, but she declined, so I called and suggested that we plan her wardrobe together. "I'm just a housewife," she said. "I'm not trying to make an impression on anybody." Doris told me that she intended to pack tennis shoes and jogging suits to wear as she toured the city. When I pointed out that the wives who would be entertaining her might be dressed more formally, she snapped that it wasn't her job to remake the company's image. As a last-ditch attempt, I proposed that she bring a pair of white kid gloves and a small evening bag for those special dinner parties she and Louis would be attending. Doris responded that her oversized saddlebag and raincoat would do just fine.

Louis's trip was not a success. Rumors filtered back through Wall Street that the French felt the American envoys were less polished than they had expected, didn't understand protocol, and seemed to show no interest in adapting to another culture. The CEO found it necessary to meet several times with his French counterparts in order to overturn this initial negative impression.

If you're reading this book in order to learn how to adjust your persona to impress any audience, you'd do well to ask your partner to follow the program with you. "Take me as I am" is a dangerous attitude for an employee, and a lethal attitude for the spouse who wants him or her to succeed.

Eagles don't want their plans to go off track because someone's spouse or partner isn't reflecting the company image.

Moles

During times of upheaval, executives sometimes hire private investigators to pose as new employees and spy on the troops. If two executives are fighting it out for leadership of a division, one might use a mole to find out which managers are loyal to him. Managers who usher in a new order of things might ask a mole to identify malcontents who are opposed to their agenda. Even as a new hire, the mole usually has no difficulty getting people to confide in him. There are two reasons for this: first, most people don't think it can be dangerous to form personal friendships at the office; second, many are enthusiastic gossipmongers—mosquitoes filled with venom, who like to swarm and sting. A request for information from the new kid on the block often elicits a tawdry recounting of who's sleeping with whom, who's using whom, and who's avenging whom.

Seduction

It's such an old dirty trick, you may be surprised to hear it still happens. Executives or moles hunting for information and blackmail material seduce secretaries or underlings. Nowadays it's just as likely to involve a long-term interoffice romance as a one-night stand. In the former case, the target of the seduction believes the romance to be genuine, while the seducer is simply establishing and maintaining an information pipeline.

Especially despicable executives encourage substance abuse to loosen tongues. The substance might be liquor or drugs or both, and the mark is usually a vulnerable type who leads a colorless life and is likely to respond to the attention. In international circles, it's practically a tradition to take deal-makers out for drinks before the contract is signed as a stealthy way of getting them to loosen their tongues and spill inside information. Women are particularly vulnerable to this tactic if they're forced to match drinks with men, who usually weigh more and thus can tolerate a lot more alcohol than they can.

At times the workplace is a battlefield, and you wouldn't want to go to war under the influence of something that weakens you. Stay alert, and don't allow yourself to be placed in a vulnerable or compromising position. As for romance, while many happily married couples met at the office, that's not the usual outcome. And extra-marital interoffice affairs are definitely off limits.

BUILD A NETWORK OF LOYAL SPIES

To protect yourself from the tricks and games going on inside an organization, it is wise to befriend the industry "bartender." There's always someone who seems to know everything about everyone, and it can be political suicide not to be on the receiving end of that information. Keep the pipeline open.

We all like to think of ourselves as being in charge of our own destiny, but all too often that's not the case. One can do everything right and still end up on the wrong side of an interoffice skirmish. How often have you seen someone's career derailed when his mentor or protector left the company? Watched a wily employee frame someone else for his mistake? Read a memo announcing that the least impressive—but best-connected—candidate in the division has been promoted ahead of several better-qualified peers? No matter how well you perform at the job, there will always be forces to contend with that are beyond your control.

If you are able to make the first move in a nasty company chess match, you can maintain your self-respect while refusing to play a losing game. Every industry is like a small town where the same faces turn up again and again—this time as colleagues, the next time as clients. The only way to survive is to opt out in a way that preserves your dignity for the next encounter.

ENEMIES NEVER DIE

What if you do open your mouth at the wrong time and make an enemy? Or an enemy from a company you worked for ages ago shows up at your new company as your peer—or worse, your boss? Machiavelli taught that "men must either be caressed or else annihilated; they will revenge themselves for small injuries.'' Start with the caressing—annihilation is a last resort!

''Caressing'' can take many forms. If the situation is serious enough, invite your foe to breakfast, lunch, or dinner. State your desire to build a better relationship or to erase past conflicts. Acknowledge his talents and strengths. You might go so far as to apologize for past misdeeds, even if you didn't commit them, and suggest that you want to start fresh, from this day forward. If your adversary has become your manager, offer cooperation and pledge your loyalty. Be big enough to adopt an eagle's attitude.

Since your goal is to defuse old animosities, watch the person's expression and listen to his words. Within three seconds you'll know where you stand just by the look on his face. If he doesn't buy it, at least you've made the effort and will be wise enough to watch your back in all future dealings with him.

My client Connie, the public relations executive from Chapter 5 who alienated her colleague Ann by using her appearance to gain attention, needed to find a way to get Ann in her corner. Bringing someone into your camp requires a different sort of ''caressing'': deliberate gossip. Connie needed to praise Ann behind her back, acknowledging her input to peers who were likely to repeat the information to Ann. To reinforce the impression that Connie admired Ann and valued her experience, I suggested that she ask Ann for advice from time to time. To prevent Connie's queries from making Ann feel used, I told Connie to complete a shared task and allow Ann to accept the credit.

It's not so easy for competitors to dislike you when you're being nice to them, especially if you are sincere. And you can't be stabbed in the back if you stand shoulder to shoulder with your enemy. But if the enemy doesn't respond after a reasonable interval, enough already. I assured Connie that if Ann wouldn't give her a chance, and if the situation deteriorated to the point where Ann was sabotaging Connie, we'd have to play a few dirty tricks of our own. There are ways to eliminate enemies without incurring their wrath. Connie could recommend Ann for a transfer to a desirable location such as London, or suggest she be given an especially prestigious account in another department. Any short-term setback that got Ann out of Connie's hair would be worth it over the long haul.

The Hit List

After reading the scenario above, it should come as no surprise that everyone, *everyone* has a hit list—including you. It may be written down, it may be kept in memory, but it exists and will be acted upon.

Everyone also has a stroke list—people they owe a favor or want to be particularly gracious toward next time they meet. Of course, this list may not be as faithfully executed as the hit list, but memories of grievances are generally more deeply etched than memories of kindness.

HIRING A HENCHMAN

Wrote Machiavelli: "Choose a cruel and able administrator, then kill him once the job is done."

When a politically astute senior executive wants to restructure his department, he may well bring in a hatchet man. This is someone with a reputation for cleaning house and then moving on, although the person may not even realize that's his role. The henchman is given power in exchange for building a case against people on the executive's hit list. After eliminating the targeted workers, the executioner finds himself transferred to a position with less responsibility and little visibility—that is, if *he* isn't terminated.

The cycle generally lasts twelve to eighteen months. It begins when an executive recognizes that his department or division is performing poorly because of personality conflicts and infighting. Or perhaps the numbers are looking weak and he must make a show of lopping off heads to impress the shareholders. So the executive pits the expendable employees against each other to raise their rivalry to the level of combat and see who will remain standing. In the process, the executive might observe someone he had previously discounted distinguish himself or herself in an unexpected way. This winner is then promoted—Peter Principle style—to the level of his own incompetence. The losers tend to leave the company in disgust—or at least the executive hopes they will. The gladiator who wins the big promotion is given the task of restructuring and reconfiguring the department—becoming a henchman. The executive sets up the assignment in such a way that the new manager will succeed in cleaning house but will eventually fail to bring about real change. (One reason he is doomed to fail is that, after firing so many employees, he has no constituency and thus no support for his reforms.) When the new numbers come in below target, the executive appears justified in diminishing the manager's responsibilities or transferring him to a less desirable assignment. The manager usually leaves under a cloud.

Alternatively, the executive might skip the soap opera and turn directly to an outsider whose mission is to engineer a turnaround (or he might see whether the above tactics work first before resorting to an outsider). Feeding the newcomer's ego with power and a rich incentive package, the executive instructs him to assess the personnel, their performances, and the structure of the business. Over time the henchman is influenced to identify the troublemakers and soft spots to which the executive leads him. The boss then empowers him to move people around or pink-slip them. Just six months later, even the henchman is sent skating. The person who carries the knife eventually gets cut by his own blade.

The catalyst for such a housecleaning isn't always something obvious, such as disappointing profits. Often it's the hiring of a new president or CEO, who wants to be surrounded by loyal followers. He enlists the aid of a troubleshooter under the guise of strategic planning, and then starts over with a clean agenda and a new team filled with deputies who owe him favors.

Oddly, the victims of this purge often move on to become the greatest successes. Disillusioned with corporate life, they develop a now-or-never attitude and start whatever business they've dreamed about all along. The wounds they suffered at the hands of their previous employer push them past the obstacles all entrepreneurial projects must overcome, and their businesses eventually flourish.

The same can't always be said for the executive who engineers all this unpleasantness. If he doesn't hire an executioner who gets in and out quickly enough, his subordinates will trace their troubles to him and mutiny. If word gets to the top of the organization, the chairman may fire the executive to preserve the company's good name. Even if the order to hire a henchman came from the chairman himself, he may choose to fire the executive who allows the henchman's activities to get too messy.

PASSED OVER FOR A PROMOTION

Sometimes you can end up on the wrong end of a dirty trick that has absolutely nothing to do with you. One example is being passed over for a promotion you deserve for no obvious reason—or for an unexpected reason that feels manufactured to you. What went wrong? Could be a power play between your manager and one of his or her competitors. Say there's enough room in the budget to promote one person. Which manager will get the chance to promote his protégé? Yours, or the politically ambitious one down the hall? You might lose the promotion, but it's really your manager who has lost political capital.

The opposite can just as easily happen—you can win a promotion that might be premature because your boss is being rewarded. We're all pawns in a larger chess game; the players we can't see are thinking several moves ahead when they move us around the board. But it does reinforce the concept that you're better off when you can hitch your wagon to someone in favor.

WHO CHANGES: THE COMPANY OR THE MAN?

One exception to the above guideline about choosing a powerful mentor is the saying, "The office doesn't change to suit the man, the man changes to suit the office." That is, hanging your hopes for a more harmonious workplace on the demise of someone you dislike or the promotion of someone you admire is not the surest path to happiness. There is only one man who can influence the profile of a company—the man at the top. If he stands for what you believe in, follow him.

It often happens that employees will work together toward the ouster of a certain manager, hoping that whatever candidate they venerate will transform their dysfunctional crew into a congenial team. This plot seldom works. More often, some unlikely comer takes over and punishes the employees who backed his competitor. Or the "nice guy" contender gets the promotion and turns into an even more vicious schemer than the previous manager. Either way, it's so easy to lose this game that it's smarter not to play. See no evil, hear no evil, speak no evil—and that means keeping your allegiances to yourself when opposing forces are battling it out.

FIRE THE HERO

This is the corporate world's version of "Only the good die young." A successful employee can lose his job to satisfy the political ambitions of a powerful mosquito. Witness the case of unlucky manager Donald.

Case Study: Donald, 42

Donald was in middle management for an information technology firm. A real worker bee, he focused so intently on doing his job well that he neglected to nurture his contacts at other companies in his industry. In fact, Donald didn't think he needed to keep his ear to the ground because he felt safe—he had just rescued a major deal that had come close to falling apart.

But Donald wasn't safe. A client of mine who had formerly worked for Donald phoned me one day in distress to say that he'd just received a call from a recruiter who asked him for leads to fill a position that sounded exactly like Donald's. Piqued, Donald's friend questioned the recruiter until he had the whole story. It turned out that Donald had a back-stabbing enemy, a colleague who was jealous of his recent coup and who had a powerful ally upstairs. Donald's nemesis, John, had called in favors from as far back as his fraternity days in order to muster enough political clout to have Donald fired by a more senior executive. Then John hired a recruiter to line up candidates to interview for Donald's position. John had also compromised Donald's reputation in the industry by bad-mouthing him to the recruiter. John's plan was to wait until after Donald had made a presentation to management outlining the techniques he had used to save the deal before giving him the boot. It was a clever way to glean his secrets and the names of his contacts before ousting him.

My client wanted Donald warned, but he didn't want to be the messenger. I suggested that the three of us make a dinner date to catch up on career news, giving me the opportunity to allude to the danger Donald faced. As it turned out, the dinner meeting was canceled. When Donald called to reschedule, he and I got into a discussion about his recent successes, and he mentioned that he had just received a magnificent job offer with a better compensation package from another company. Donald said he wasn't considering the offer because his future at his current company was so rosy! Plus, he was just a month away from receiving his annual bonus.

That did it. I told Donald the word on the street was that he was on the verge of being ousted; I urged him to accept the job offer in order to take the lead and outsmart his firm. We planned his resignation together, and the next day he waltzed into his boss's office and shocked him by quitting. Acting as if he knew nothing about his imminent termination, Donald played the part of the winner, talking about his positive experience with the company and his wish for a continued relationship. I instructed Donald to delay asking for his bonus money, but to mention it casually the next time he and his supervisor spoke, as if he took it completely for granted that they would pay him what he was due.

THE GOOD RAT

Here's a dirty trick that's worth playing yourself. Remember Donald's friend, his former employee? I followed up on Donald's resignation by turning the friend into a so-called "good rat," someone whose gossip can do some good.

I called the friend—my client—and told him the three of us should reschedule our meal, but this time as a celebration dinner. Pretending the whole event was a happy coincidence, I told my client I hadn't even had the chance to fill Donald in on what his firm had in store. Instead, I told my client that the recruiter had been misled and had gotten the story all wrong: Donald wasn't being ousted, he was resigning to become a partner in a rival software venture. But before Donald could resign, his boss had found out he was negotiating with a competitor and wanted the perverse pleasure of giving him his walking papers before he had a chance to quit. (Yes, I fudged the account, but I was trying to put a positive spin on Donald's departure and make his rival in the company look ridiculous to the recruiters so they'd distrust the schemer's future stories.)

As I had hoped, my client was ecstatic at this turn of events and vowed to call back the recruiter and set him straight. Most likely the recruiter would then pass the gossip along to others and start a positive rumor about Donald and his triumph, transforming his reputation from victim to victor.

The benefit of building a loyal constituency throughout your career is that one of your allies can counter the effects of an enemy who is bad-mouthing you. Whoever hears about it can reverse the stream by talking about you positively behind your back. Even more effective is asking your defenders to use humor to defuse the gossip at the source, putting the misbehaving party in the hot seat by joking with him about his vendetta. He won't retaliate against you because he isn't aware you've engineered this show of support.

BRIBERY

You may be aware of another trick recognized by Machiavelli. "It is customary for those who wish to gain the favor of a prince to endeavor to do so by offering him gifts of those things which they hold most precious, or in which they know him to take especial delight."

Bribery is one of those strategies that qualifies as a dirty trick only if you're not the one doing it! Of course, not all boodle is benign. The most common form involves lavish entertaining or gifts far exceeding the widely accepted $25 limit: ski trips, Florida vacations, Caribbean cruises. One former client, a company president, received an all-expense-paid trip out West with his family every year from a company that wanted to keep his business. And we're always reading about one outfit or another bribing a company or the government to be awarded a contract. When the best man, or the fairest bid, doesn't win, you have to wonder what might be happening behind the scenes.

Whether or not you approve, you'll probably be forced to play the game yourself someday. Your competitors may curry favor with an influential person by sending him to the British Open at St. Andrew's in Scotland or inviting him to spend a week at their Mediterranean villa. It's tough to beat that kind of competition, but I strongly recommend that you draw the line when it comes to payola.

THE NAUGHTY GOOD RAT

There is another definition of the good rat, the kind I urge my clients not to become. I speak of the loyal employee who uncovers illegal or disloyal activity among his colleagues and feels compelled to bring the wrongdoing to management's attention. Sure, management may appreciate having this information, but they may not appreciate your being the messenger. The naughty good rat ends up dying in a trap set by his managers, who are embarrassed to have him around. They love to play a dirty trick on a good rat, if they can catch him.

Michael Lewis, columnist for the *New York Times,* says that loyalty is more often an excuse than a virtue, and he may be right. Good rats are often more interested in calling attention to themselves than in righting corporate wrongs. Like a kindergartner, the rat is looking for some sort of reward for tattling. My priority is strategic planning for the long-term success of my clients' careers, not the ethics of their colleagues. I suggest that, if a client discovers a breach he can't abide, he ought to alert management indirectly, so that his identity isn't tied to the revelation.

If you doubt the risk, consider the fate of the whistleblower who may be stepping into a bigger quagmire. The person he's relating the story to may be involved in the problem, and he will soon discover that it's common for companies to turn on the squealers.

To maintain a clear conscience while staying away from the mayhem, leak the information judiciously and anonymously. Submit an unsigned note or find a well-known curmudgeon to carry the message for you. Resist the urge to tip off the press; keep the problem private. You're not a troublemaker, you're an eagle.

SCHADENFREUDE

Definition: *pleasure derived from the misfortunes of others.* As an eagle you may have these feelings when someone you know is playing dirty tricks and is finally caught and punished. But don't relish the troubles of others, no matter how much the bad guy may deserve to be brought down. We all have a dark side, but eagles know enough to stay out of the shadows, to fly toward the sun. It's part of adopting a macro, rather than micro, point of view.

If you sense you're unjustly becoming the fall guy for someone else's dirty tricks and are about to become the object of such feelings, hold your head high and continue to do your best. If, on the other hand, you sense that your detractors are doing more than snickering behind your back, sniff around until you've decided what mischief they may be up to. Then bring up the subject obliquely to observe the offender's reaction. A guilty response means you should consider taking action.

THEY'RE OUT TO GET YOU

Diverted Mail and Memos

Years ago, Jane Trahey described a scenario in her book *Thursday's at Nine* that's a dirty trick still being used: executives who wanted to cripple an arrogant employee's career delayed, diverted, or never sent key memos. Some scoundrels even composed fake memos about fictional meetings or printed out modified versions of memos about real meetings, changing the time or location.

To protect yourself from such nonsense, communicate regularly with the members of your team to confirm goals and gatherings.

It's smart to protect yourself by using your spy network, if you want to survive these days.

Being There Is Half the Battle

If you're left out of a meeting, it not only deprives you of information but slights you among your peers. This can undermine your ability to perform at capacity because people under fire tend to lose allies, who step away in an effort to distance themselves from a sinking ship.

Psychodynamics provides a way out. At a later date, when the results of the meeting are discussed and allies are present, mention that you're sorry you weren't included in the meeting because you'd prefer to keep on top of the matter at hand. An alternative is to say you'd like to be included in future meetings to stay up to speed on the subject. Firmly state that you know this won't happen again. Don't whine, go on the offensive. Your comment will embarrass the party who excluded you, and it will force him to make his move or to change his tactics.

Upward Evaluations

A recent trend among hip organizations is to ask employees to judge the performance of their managers. The workers either fill out a supposedly anonymous form or allow themselves to be interviewed by a human resources staffer on a confidential basis. The dangers are obvious. Questionnaires can be surreptitiously marked to identify the employee who fills them out, and the human resources staffer who inputs the data can fail in his effort to protect each evaluator's identity. If the boss being evaluated is powerful enough, he can pressure the human resources department to name the people who wrote the most negative comments.

Even when the evaluations run smoothly, employees can get burned. One monomaniacal manager entrapped his subordinates by calling each one into his office and pretending he had been told every criticism each employee had made. Convinced, the staffers proceeded to hang themselves by blubbering about their comments.

Denying a Raise

If you're denied a pay raise, or given a smaller raise than your peers, it may be a sign that your performance is below par. But in the world of dirty tricks, there could be another reason: a boss does it because he thinks he can get away with it.

What I mean is that troublemakers can smell a mortgage a mile away. If an employee is responsible for his or her family and its endless bills, if an unmarried worker is caring for his or her sick parent, if his job is the difference between making it and going under, the company monster will take advantage. Like the gloating executive who was able to hire an impressive woman for less money than she was worth, managers often lowball pay increases to see if the employee will resign himself to less than he expects. If it works, the manager has saved himself some budget money.

As I discussed in Chapter 6, you must adopt a walk-away attitude even if you don't actually have one. Project the temperament of someone who will stand up for what he deserves, and you may not have to.

Reduction of Privileges

Unlike offering a puny salary increase, taking away privileges is usually management's way of sending a message that the employee should leave the company. The wake-up call may take the form of:

- Restricting the employee's use of company credit cards
- Exclusion from industry events or conferences
- Limiting travel and expense accounts
- Downgrading travel from first or business class to coach
- Moving the employee to a smaller office or less convenient parking space
- Restricting use of the executive dining room or health club

Of course, if these measures are taken as part of a companywide cost-cutting spree, there's no need to fear you'll be singled out for termination. But even so, a company that cuts privileges ultimately cuts staff. Punch up your résumé and consider jumping ship.

WATCH WHO YOU'RE TALKING TO

You're Never Alone

One of the strangest phenomena I've observed is that, when executives are in the company of people they don't know or respect, they sometimes behave as if they were alone. I've seen them pick up a secretary's phone and discuss confidential information in front of him or her—no worries. Or jabber on about sensitive topics in elevators or on public transportation.

Once when I was flying home from a Caribbean holiday, a man wearing an expensive business suit and carrying a briefcase labeled with the name of a Big Six accounting firm sat down near me in coach. It didn't take much imagination to realize that he was handling some offshore business. Perhaps assuming that he was surrounded by unsophisticated tourists, the accounting exec used his own cellular phone to call his office right after the flight attendant had asked us not to use such devices, and loudly instructed an assistant to "be a good slave" and bury an expense report in an international account. I was amazed. Apparently I wasn't the only one, because not two weeks later a friend called and told me the same story. Realizing that this situation needed to be nipped in the bud and wanting to protect my contacts at the firm, I suggested that he call the top executives to tell them the story. The company comptroller traced the incident and disciplined the executive.

Executives who speak freely in front of other people's secretaries do so at their own peril. The chairman's administrative assistant can wield more power than three vice presidents put together, and tends to be fiercely loyal. It's normal for these assistants to identify with the power level of their bosses, and pass along information to enhance that power. They also want to prove to vice presidents and other administrative assistants that they serve the most influential executive in the company. So they swap gossip with other secretaries, who pass it along to their own prominent managers.

Blind Ads

Do you really want to find out what employees think of your company? An executive with a major publishing firm used to place enticing advertisements for nonexistent positions in the Help Wanted section of newspapers and trade journals each year during budget planning time. The ads helped him discover what his competitors were paying because applicants were asked to reveal their current salaries. If any of his own employees responded, he considered them disloyal and put them out to pasture.

When answering a blind ad, always keep in mind the possibility that it may have been placed by your own company. Don't divulge your salary, even if guaranteed confidentiality. If you must, give a range that includes all of your benefits, which can translate to an amount as high as 50% of your yearly pay.

Illegal Questions

It is unlawful to ask a job candidate questions about his age, race, religion, or marital status. Still, interviewers have found ways around these restrictions. Asking when you might prefer to take vacation can tell them what religion you are. They find out your age by asking seemingly harmless questions about your children. Mention you have a son who's getting married next month and you've talked yourself right out of a job—the interviewer assumes you're nearing fifty and will soon be drawing on the pension plan.

Don't underestimate the lengths a crafty manager will go to in weeding out older employees. One night an aircraft industry chairman called the company's CEO and told him to fire everyone over fifty. "Are you crazy?" asked the CEO. "Some of the best people in this company are over fifty and I hired them."

"It doesn't matter," replied the chairman. "Buy them off, but just get rid of them so we don't have to put them on the pension plan."

There's more. As an interviewer judges whether you'd be a good fit in his department, he may want to know your attitude about work in general. To ferret out this information, he might prompt you to talk by saying that he worked his way through school—how did you manage? Your answer indicates your level of financial independence. People who make the mistake of explaining that they too have had to overcome obstacles are often given more obstacles to overcome. Check your candor and downplay any dramas in your past. Aim for a self-confident demeanor that will tell the interviewer you expect to be treated fairly—regardless of your circumstances.

Testing, Testing . . .

Here's a charming ploy: a division head gives you the good news that you're one of the top candidates for promotion to management. The hitch is that, as part of the final screening process, you are required to take a diagnostic test.

The truth may be just the opposite; your manager has heard a rumor that you're having a breakdown and wants to confirm it before sending you packing. Even if the company's brass are thinking of promoting you, the fact that they have asked for a management test means (a) they don't trust their own judgment, and (b) regardless of the outcome, they will now be apprised of your psychological weaknesses.

There's little you can do; you certainly can't refuse to take the test. It does help, however, to give upbeat, positive answers to the questions.

This dirty trick can also be played by sending an employee to an off-site seminar. The company may go so far as to hire spies to report back on how much you drink, what you say, how you behave. Again, they may use this information to confirm or deny a rumor, or to ascertain whether you're refined enough to promote to management. If indeed a job is like a role in a major theatrical production, think of yourself as always being on stage. Never go out of character in front of any audience that pays your salary!

MOVE 'EM AND DUMP 'EM

There's always a secret agenda when a company relocates its offices. It may be something as simple as cost cutting—starting a new lease in a less expensive area to reduce overhead. But a more diabolical scenario is to start fresh with a new staff without having to engage in mass terminations. The company announces a move to another region and invites employees to decide whether they'll come along. A high percentage leave the company because their families or other commitments force them to remain in town.

One company that pulled this off moved its Northeast offices to the Southeast, and its Northwest offices to the Southwest. There were no other firms in the industry at either of the new locations. Suspecting they might lose their jobs after they moved and then be stranded in an area with no other opportunities, almost all the employees resigned, freeing the company to hire new workers at lower salaries.

Sometimes a company doesn't even follow through on the move—it simply waits a decent interval before announcing that the city has come up with an incentives package to keep the company from leaving. Again, it hires a whole new staff—younger and less compensated.

If you elect to follow your company to a new location, get all contingencies in writing. That includes a clause stating that, if your company "rightsizes" after the move, it will pay for you to move back home.

DUPLICATE FILES

On occasion employees ought to review the file that is kept on them by the company. The law in some states says that the company must allow employees free access to all materials found in this file. Companies can avoid complying by keeping double files: one for your eyes and one for theirs. It's simple enough to accomplish, and nearly impossible for you to detect or prove. Unfortunately there's nothing to do about it but to be aware that it happens, especially when someone is building a case against you.

"ON THE BEACH"

Executives who sense they may be let go sometimes make the big mistake of calling the recruiter who placed them in their current position, hoping to find a new lead. Wrong! The exec may have liked the recruiter, but he must remember that the recruiter was paid by the executive's company, and that's where his loyalty lies. The recruiter sees this as a three-way opportunity:

1. An assignment to fill the executive's current job.
2. A chance to curry favor with the executive's company by squealing on him.
3. A candidate who can be placed in a new assignment.

The executive makes the call because he is worried he'll end up "on the beach," but the phone call itself insures he'll have nothing to do but walk the shore in no time.

The executive can rely on the recruiter only if he's been building the relationship all along. If you've made a friend of a recruiter who's placed you in a big job, he knows you'll take him along with you and give him assignments as your career progresses. His allegiance is to you, not to your company. But if you call him only when you're in trouble, you're asking for *more* trouble.

Before making the call, consider the risks.

There is no such thing as a private conversation on an office phone. Most people would be amazed at how prevalent wiretapping, along with other surveillance methods such as hidden cameras, is in corporate America. Electronic mail is not secure; nor is the information on your computer's hard drive. As with office searches, assume your communications are being monitored and restrict your personal business to the home.

When the time comes for an exit interview, be discreet. Keep your discussion brief and positive. Don't allow the interviewer to use you for research by pumping you for information about your boss or department. Remember that the notes the human resources person takes at the interview will go back to the boss and into your file, and be read years down the road when you ask your old boss for a recommendation. There's a lot of truth to what people say in exit interviews. Sometimes a departing employee uses the meeting as an opportunity to wipe the slate clean, revealing that Staffer A was blamed for a mistake he knows Staffer B actually made. Others feel free to air their grievances, especially if they're leaving the company because they failed to advance or were treated badly. Take it for granted that *every word you say in an exit interview will get back to your department head.*

OUTPLACEMENT DECEIT

An entire department is eliminated and its workers are "downsized" right out of the company. All is not lost, says the human resources department—the company will provide outplacement services for all of you. Free. Take advantage. We're here to help.

Really? Outplacement sounds like a nice idea, but you don't get something for nothing. Outplacement firms sell their services to companies that are cutting jobs by saying that they will protect the company from being sued by the terminated workers. How? I knew a CEO who pumped the outplacement company for damning personal information about the exiting employees so that when these people threatened to sue the company for wrongful dismissal he could use the information to dissuade them from the suit.

Workers on the verge of unemployment are a vulnerable lot who tend to confide heavily in people offering help. Outplacement counselors hear about family problems, alcoholism—you name it. They also conduct psychological tests to determine what sort of position would be the best fit; less ethical counselors feed the personal information they've gleaned from these tests back to the company to use for blackmail.

THREE-SECOND OVERVIEW

Life isn't always fair, as you've discovered in this chapter. You may not like what goes on behind the scenes, but you're not being paranoid if you sense that something seems amiss. It probably is!

In the final chapter, we'll put the finishing touches on how you can make the right impression and fly with the eagles while still retaining your principles!

9

An Eagle's Profile

INSPIRE AND LEAD: POWER SECRET #10

There are eagles at every socioeconomic level. These are the people who enrich every day of their lives and the lives of others because of an ability to inspire people to reveal their own gifts and make contributions. To be a real winner means to bring these qualities to business, family, community, and the world. In this regard, every one of us has the obligation to be gracious and generous to others, and the capacity for great leadership.

For ambitious people, social life and business life are inseparable. A prestigious position at a leading company can pave the way to memberships in private clubs and philanthropic boards, and those memberships can in turn boost your career. Thus, any agenda you might pursue in business must consider the social angle. People who occupy the business level you're shooting for are more likely to accept you if you're a member of their social set, and vice versa.

Is there a chicken-egg problem here? Not necessarily. Usually people achieve some degree of business success first; once they've risen within the corporation and are exposed to a more sophisticated group, they start to form social goals based on the lifestyle enjoyed by their new peers. Often it's a world they've never been exposed to before, and they have no notion of how to advance within it.

Honestly, being accepted at private clubs and other exclusive places isn't as mysterious as it looks. Difficult, yes, but not mysterious. The first rule for getting in anywhere is to look and act the part, and that requires following my program to determine the members' values and behavior in order to emulate them. Then, like a politician running for office, you have to hit the campaign trail, kissing babies while telling each constituent what he wants to hear. If you win enough votes, you're in; if you don't, you probably won't have another chance to gain admission to that particular club. In that case, there are plenty of other ways to achieve your social goals, and I'll explain those later in the chapter. In the meantime, consider how joining an exclusive group made the difference in one eagle's career.

Case Study: Maryann, 34

Maryann's career in retail sales had stalled when she came to me for help. We determined that her biggest obstacle was her lower-middle-class roots; she just didn't fit in with colleagues a level above her. At the same time, Maryann was discontented with her industry because its long hours limited her ability to pursue any social life at all. Her company kept stores open later and later each year to stay competitive, and Maryann was stuck working twelve-hour shifts every time a staffer failed to show up for work. Her inability to take weekends off meant she had no time to schuss down her favorite ski slopes, further limiting her social options.

To begin, I suggested she take a summer share in a beachside house with other friends at her office. (People who don't live near the coast have the option of taking a share at a lakeside or ski resort.) This seaside community was a hotbed of young professionals. She took me up on the idea, and while socializing there, Maryann befriended someone in her own company who then helped her move up to the position of buyer.

As Maryann had anticipated, being promoted didn't overcome all her objections to retailing. But rather than commencing an immediate job search, she took my advice to pursue some sort of involvement in her other great passion: the ballet. She joined a volunteer group whose work benefitted a local ballet company, sending out mailers, calling potential subscribers, and attending benefit parties. Through her fund-raising efforts, Maryann became comfortable with the more affluent group of volunteers, and discovered an interest in the stock market.

Contacts in hand, Maryann landed a job with a prominent brokerage house. Her new acquaintances became her clients and she rewarded their trust with hefty profits. That cemented their association, and soon she found herself being invited to private dinner parties. Maryann told me she still felt a bit uncomfortable at these events, so I urged her to take up sports like sailing, tennis, and golf so that her pursuits and experience would more closely match those of her new companions. Soon afterward she met her future husband while she was a guest at the home of one of her new friends. Happy ending: Maryann and her husband asked for and received transfers to the Rocky Mountain area where they now live, taking full advantage of the ski slopes nearby.

Maryann's story illustrates an encouraging fact about expanding your socio-business horizons: the best way to begin is to volunteer for a cause you care about, and remember: *charities have no membership requirements.* I stress the fact that the organization you choose must be one whose goals genuinely touch your heart—insincerity won't get you far, no matter how good a performer you may be.

VOLUNTEERISM

When I talk to clients about volunteerism, they often confuse it with philanthropy—making contributions to the arts or other charitable organizations. Indeed, writing those big checks is an effective way to draw attention to yourself, and the organizations who receive the benefit of your largesse certainly won't complain. But I stress service, the donation of precious time. Philanthropic organizations need time just as much as they need money, and it is your frequent presence that will enhance your social opportunities.

Working together with others who share an interest in a worthy cause has a way of dissolving class barriers.

The opportunities that can come from participating in a philanthropic organization are astonishing. One unlikely example is the time I met the Dalai Lama as a direct result of my involvement with an international charity. The people you meet through charity work tend to invite you to take advantage of their personal and business associations. If they're off to meet the Dalai Lama, you might be granted an audience. If tonight's dinner guest is the CEO of a company you long to work for, you might get the informal interview of a lifetime.

All the same, I don't want to stress the notion of engaging in charity work just to advance in social or business life. It's simply one benefit from an undertaking that is good for the soul. Even Machiavelli, whom I have quoted repeatedly in the previous chapter, wrote that "so far as [a leader] is intelligent, he knows that his social nature and need involves a code of conduct which is, of course, a moral code, and that to some degree each should strive for the welfare of all." People who work for the good of others will in some unknown way and on some unknown day be rewarded for their altruism.

The only aspect of volunteerism that insinuates a desire for admission to a private club is the solicitation of an endorsement by one of its members. Frankly, there is little any of us can do to elicit that honor. It doesn't do any good to campaign for it—such obvious social climbing is considered distasteful. Instead, give more than you expect in return.

Ripples

The ripple effect became a reality for me, and it can become a reality for you, too: a reputable nonprofit organization gives one award or special recognition and another group follows suit.

When the Boy Scouts needed career training for teenage members of the Explorer Scouts, I recruited six corporate executives to assist me. To express my gratitude, I proposed them for membership on the Explorers' board of directors. We arranged training meetings for the youngsters with speakers from a variety of industries. It soon became obvious that training several thousand young people was going to be a monumental task, so I invited the Junior League to step in and design a program to continue the counseling. The following year, I recruited a Pepsi Cola executive to serve on the board of the Greater New York Council of the Boy Scouts with sixty-five other tycoons of industry. Subsequently, I was invited to join the board myself. In 1993, the Scouts honored me with their Explorers' Leadership Award.

My acceptance speech for the Leadership Award moved a member of the audience to recommend me as a speaker for the Million Dollar Roundtable, an exclusive group of insurance executives. Who could have guessed that a few words of thanks could lead to another opportunity?

This story demonstrates not just the rewards of humanitarianism but the benefits of good communication skills. Becoming a convincing speaker makes you even more of an asset to a philanthropic group. You may be asked to propose a course of action to the board or to make a public speech on behalf of the organization. See Chapter 7 for more details on speechwriting and public speaking.

THE PRIVATE CLUB

The process leading up to the point where an ambitious person can take the leap to membership in a private club is a long one. It involves achieving some success in business, refining manners and image to go higher in the corporation, and establishing a social presence through volunteerism and community service. Finally, it may become clear that belonging to a particular sport club or supper club will enhance both business and social opportunities, and it's time to take the plunge.

Throughout this book I've addressed the problem of wanting to enhance your life, whether that means earning a promotion, being better paid, or pursuing stimulating outside activities. Even people from wealthy families sometimes need guidance to maximize their comfort level and find a peer group to work and socialize with. Consider the following story:

Case Study: James, 32

James, the scion of a prominent family, had moved to a city where he had few acquaintances outside of his parents' peers and contacts. Interested in excelling at his new job in the reinsurance industry, he worked long hours and tried not to focus on his lack of social outlets. In fact, he was so private and unassuming that his colleagues had no idea about his background.

In time, the support staff got wind of James's affluence through the CEO's gossipy secretary. They resented his connections and began hazing him mercilessly. They neglected to forward his telephone calls, delayed his mail, and left his name off key interoffice memos. He came to me for advice about handling these bozos.

I suggested he ignore the mosquitoes who were stinging him and focus on filling his life with fellow eagles. Perhaps he could commiserate with other privileged young people who had received similar treatment. I suggested he use his family connections to take out junior memberships in several private clubs: sports, social, and civic. The variety would ensure his exposure to a cross section of people at his level. James took my advice, and as he established rapport with his peers, they urged him to explore a career move to investment banking. James made the move and found that in his new company he was appreciated, not punished, for his background.

Social agendas aside, the choice to seek membership in a private club should be motivated by a desire to be surrounded by stimulating people whose company you'd enjoy—just as it was for James. Once you've targeted a club you feel would fulfill that need, you must convince the admissions committee that you'll fulfill their needs as well. Their purpose in life is not to admit you to their club but to screen you as a candidate who will add something to the group. This is one reason to pursue community service beforehand; it's a way of demonstrating your desire to give of yourself, not just suck the members dry of favors and contacts.

Before approaching the admissions committee, consider the fact that there are four basic ways to get ahead in any context:

1. Intelligence
2. Humanitarianism
3. Physical prowess or attractiveness
4. Connections

You must possess some combination of these attributes for an admissions committee to accept you. For example, if you're aiming for membership in a tennis club and you're a whiz with a racket, you'll have a better chance—members will want the opportunity to play their favorite game with someone who challenges them to improve. Thus, it's wise to maximize your strengths before you even look for a sponsor.

To begin the admissions process, most clubs require you to have a sponsor and two or three letters of recommendation from club members. The sponsor hosts informal get-togethers to introduce you to key members of the club. Then you (and your spouse, if applicable) meet with an admissions committee whose members check your credentials, both personal and financial. Finally they take a vote. If you're accepted, you can expect to be invited to become a member of other clubs, since many club members have multiple affiliations. These contacts, plus your contributions and attributes, build your reputation as a well-rounded member of the community.

Unfortunately, some clubs still exclude certain people because of their race or religion. The clubs' private status exempts them from laws that keep public organizations from making decisions on this basis. Rather than dwell on the injustice of the system, you'd do well to remember the main reason you're seeking club membership in the first place: to surround yourself with people whose values are similar to yours. If you focus on this need, it's unlikely you'd even want to belong to a club that would exclude you on the basis of your race or religion—it makes no sense. Such clubs have a reputation that precedes them, one that applicants know about before they even apply. My suggestion is, unless you're on a mission to right wrongs, don't waste your scarce time and precious spirit on fruitless crusades. Apply to a club filled with people you respect and whose company you would enjoy.

MOVING TO A NEW COMMUNITY

The application process described above relies on your friendship with at least three members of a club—not an easy feat if you're new in town. One idea is to take advantage of your corporate network to find a sponsor, but that's most likely to succeed if you or your spouse holds a Great Big Job. (Remember the list of attributes that get people ahead? Members of a club would overlook a top executive's lack of friends because of the prestige factor associated with his business stature.) The rest of us are better off pursuing friendships on our own. The reality is that, unless Daddy owns the store, it takes up to three years for the average newcomer to assimilate into a community and build the relationships necessary to apply to a private club.

New arrivals should join civic groups in order to meet people who belong to the local clubs. And regardless of how long a woman has lived in her community, she should consider joining an organization like the Junior League. Part of the Junior League's attraction is the way the group reaches out to members from other cities who have moved to their area.

CHANGING YOUR IMAGE IN YOUR OLD COMMUNITY

If you've followed my guidelines to change your image in order to rise in the business or social world, you might find it difficult to be accepted by a different group from the one with whom you've socialized so long. Either these people don't know you, or they think of you as someone who is not in their sphere.

As with my clients who use strategies to make their managers reevaluate them, you can make more sophisticated people think of you differently. Expose them to the new you. Court them by including them in an event, such as a benefit for charity. Ask them to join you when you are taking an important client to lunch, dinner, a concert, or the theater. Build rapport and the need for reciprocity, and your courtesies will most likely be returned.

You must be more of a giver than a taker to earn people's regard.

It's your consideration for others that makes them want to include rather than exclude you.

IF NOT CLUBS, WHAT?

Not everyone is meant for the exclusive club scene, and not everyone wants to be. Spiritual groups offer companionship with people who agree on a particular religious philosophy, and these groups have no membership requirements other than a willingness to believe. And except for paying dues and writing a check, you have fulfilled the requirements for membership in your university's alumni association simply by graduating.

Many companies will pay employees' membership fees in business associations. I think that executives who claim they're too busy to participate in industry groups are really missing out on opportunities for friendships, job leads, and underground information.

One social outlet that people tend to overlook is the political organization, either the type that raises money for a party or one that promotes the career of a single candidate. What a rare chance to talk politics with acquaintances and not get into a rip-roaring argument!

Any activity you enjoy can provide a place to meet people with shared interests. Take an extension course at a local university, swim at the Y, coach your child's Little League team, join a bridge group—it just takes a little motivation and imagination. Throughout, identify the personality traits of people you're interested in so that you can enhance the likelihood of bonding with them.

WHEN BUSINESS AND SOCIAL WORLDS COLLIDE

Some of the biggest business mistakes happen when employees don't draw a line between their business and social lives. As I said earlier, it is indeed a socio-business world. But it's important to understand exactly what that means. At a certain point in your career, your business and social lives will begin to enhance each other. That doesn't mean, however, that you should become intimate with your business acquaintances or go into business deals with your lifelong friends.

As employees work longer and longer hours, they are less likely to see any difference between their business life and their social life. They make personal friends at the office and go out with them after work and on weekends. The few childhood or college friends they still have may live too far away to keep in close touch. For a while, the business friendships may run smoothly, giving the office a warm, family feeling. Eventually, though, one or more of these business friendships blows up, leaving awkwardness in its wake. Worse, there will always be the worry that one estranged friend will use personal confidences to undermine the career of the other.

Except for relationships that come about when shared experiences, interests, and personality traits cause two people to form a deep bond, most friendships are transitory. They generally last three years, perhaps five—as long as the circumstances that brought the people together remain stable. When the circumstances change, many friendships can't adjust, and they fall apart. Worse yet, office friendships tend not to fade away but to detonate; issues of shifting rank and reward may cause a level of bitterness that can't be reconciled.

I'm not saying that it's always deadly to become intimate with a business friend; never to allow yourself to get close to someone you work with every day would be inhuman. But as a rule it's best to keep things on a more superficial level. Try not to reveal personal information about family, health, or finances. These details aren't really relevant to building camaraderie among colleagues. Keeping an invisible barrier between you and your associates becomes even more important as you move up in the organization, when there's even more at stake. The phrase "familiarity breeds contempt" is one cliché worth remembering.

COURTESIES TO YOUR BOSS

Here's a problem most etiquette books don't have an answer for. To what extent do you involve your boss in your social life? Do you give him or her a holiday gift? Do you invite her to your daughter's wedding? Do you send a note when you hear of a death in her family?

The answer to all of these questions is *yes*. Show your boss the utmost level of courtesy. Almost every boss plays a vital role in your life and appreciates your acknowledgment for his efforts on your behalf.

There are certain limitations. It is not considered good form to invite your boss and his wife to dinner in your home, unless it's a company party. In fact, if there's an occasion that demands business entertaining, the safest choice is a restaurant or hotel. Do invite your boss, and his spouse or significant other, to public-private events such as a wedding. If you report to more than one person, be sure to invite both parties.

If your boss accepts the invitation, try to seat him with people of equal stature. You won't earn points for including him if he is seated with strangers with whom he has little in common and ends up watching the clock all night.

Gifts

It's difficult to choose the right gift without overstepping the boundaries of good taste. The best choices are practical and possibly edible—not too personal or too expensive. Here are some ideas:

The day before a dinner party, or when you want to express congratulations for a promotion, or when it's courteous to show concern for an illness:

- Flowers, chocolates, or candies
- A holiday candle or a simple seasonal decorative item
- A book or silver bookmark with engraved initials
- Yearly goods such as a calendar or an address book
- Family games such as backgammon or checkers
- A subscription to a family magazine such as *National Geographic*
- A donation to a charity in the recipient's name
- Items related to the person's profession

- Music tapes or CDs
- A crystal paperweight

PERSONAL NOTES

Sophisticated eagles enjoy dashing off personal notes to compatriots. These short-but-personal messages are handwritten on bonded note cards or Monarch-size paper. (Business stationery information is covered in Chapter 6.) In the left corner, or centered at the top of the page, is a monogram from one of the styles offered by such fine stationers, engravers, and paper goods specialists as Tiffany, Cartier, Dempsey & Carroll, Mrs. John L. Strong, Merrimade, Crane's, Pineider of Italy, Armorial and Benneton of France, and Smythson of Bond Street. The custom-printing prices vary from moderate to costly, depending on whether the writer's name or monogram is embossed, engraved, raised ink, or laser-printed, and the back of the envelope includes your printed address (not your name).

SOCIO-BUSINESS PET PEEVES

After years of counseling clients, I've discovered that most opportunities are lost when people make the same few mistakes over and over. Because socioeconomic snubs are subtle, my clients don't always know where they went wrong—thus the innocent repetition of faux pas. Some of the following pet peeves involve behavior my clients and I have observed among thoughtless people; others are gaffes we all make from time to time.

Professional Friendship Does Not Extend to the Second Level

That is, you can't ask a professional acquaintance to do a favor for a friend or relative. If someone makes this request of you, don't feel you have to make an excuse. Simply say, "I'm very sorry, but I'm not able to extend that courtesy at this time." If they're sophisticated, they'll get the message. Shyer types can also insist they're too busy.

This rule also extends to personal networking. It's not proper to ask a professional acquaintance to help you meet one of his or her contacts. If a colleague wants to help, he'll volunteer.

Friends Promote Each Other's Careers at Their Own Peril

This may sound like an odd rule, but it's a genuinely dangerous practice. We all want to benefit from networking, and we should. But if you stick your neck out far enough to get a friend a job, you've taken on a ticklish responsibility. If the friend doesn't like the job, he or she will blame you. If the friend proves to be a less than impressive employee, your contact will blame you. The only positive outcome is if the friend excels, but if he manages to eclipse you, you'll feel resentful. It's smarter to offer the use of your contacts to help a friend get in the door, then leave him to win the job (or other benefit) on his own merits.

The same applies where a business friend needs to be bailed out of a serious situation—such as being caught breaking the law. There's an old Asian saying that you should never save someone's life because he can never repay you. The modern version is "No good deed goes unpunished." So think it through before you play Superman. Your friend may never stop resenting you for the one-up position you've gained in his life.

Never Use a Friend's Business Contact Without Including Him in the Interaction

If a friend introduces you to an influential contact, the friend must remain the link. I've heard people gush: "I had a great conversation with my friend's contact! We bonded! We're pals now!" Not so. Even if you eventually strike up your own relationship with the friend's contact, be sure to mention your encounters to the friend who introduced you. Your first loyalty is to the friendship.

Group Interactions Should Not Turn Exclusionary

This behavior makes me angry. I'll see a group talking, then two of the people turn to each other and conduct a private conversation, sometimes in another language. Sometimes they'll even bring social invitations into the discussion in front of people they don't intend to include. Or another person will approach the group and try to join the conversation, but the group won't permit it. They'll actually close the circle further, keeping their backs to the poor newcomer, who slinks away, rejected. This is the conduct of mosquitoes.

Most common is when dinner partners don't realize it's proper etiquette to devote equal time to the people on either side. Sometimes people don't know any better, but just as often it's because they're interested in the more powerful of their dinner companions. One time I watched an executive ignore the women on both sides of him in favor of the dignitary seated across the table. When the people on the women's far sides turned to their other dinner partners, the women had no one to talk to. Little did the boor know he had alienated the powerful spouse of the CEO whose favor he had been currying for several months.

Whether you're the host or a guest, there's no room for memory lapses at a business soiree. Keep a Who's Who card on business associates with vital statistics on their career history, family status, education, political affiliations, favorite sports and hobbies, and other details. Review the data before the event so you don't blank out in a conversation with your dinner partner.

Invitations Deserve a Response

The worn-out excuse that we're all so busy we forget to RSVP on time will not pass muster. It's just plain *rude!* Too often hosts find themselves on the phone for hours trying to determine how many guests they can expect. Even people who wouldn't think of failing to respond to a personal invitation regularly ignore the RSVP on business invitations. Eagles don't apply different standards of behavior to their business and social lives. They behave appropriately, whether the invitation is sent by a personal friend or a public relations assistant. They know it merits a prompt answer.

Following attendance at a private social event also requires a courtesy. Send a thank-you note! You might also send the host a small gift, or schedule a return invitation. An affair held for your benefit, such as a get-acquainted party given by your club sponsor, rates a larger gesture—perhaps tickets to a sporting or cultural event.

Everyone's time is precious. Sometimes we can forget that we're not the only ones who are too busy. We'll break a lunch date less than a day ahead of time, or try to make a last-minute date without giving an explanation for the lack of notice. We neglect to return phone calls—whether business or personal—within two days. Of course, everyone has an inner circle of friends who understand these breaches, and that's their role. People outside this circle, however, won't be so understanding.

We are not alone. People who dine by themselves or walk on the street alone forget that they're surrounded by people: strangers. Gracious manners shouldn't end because you're not in the company of acquaintances. In fact, ignoring etiquette in public can lead to some lamentable coincidences. One man who was late to an important lunch meeting at which he hoped to sign a lucrative deal yelled at a woman who was walking too slowly ahead of him. After he was seated at the restaurant, the same woman joined his table; it turned out she was a top executive of the company with which he wanted to make the deal. You can guess the outcome.

We should respect the needs of strangers. I've observed business executives reading oversized newspapers at fine restaurants, obscuring the view of other customers. Cellular phones cause more than their share of irritations. Diners bellow into them at restaurants, making it difficult for others to hear themselves think. These same people bash into other pedestrians while walking and talking, or hit other cars while driving and talking.

Negativism

This is a toxic trait, whether in the business or social arena. Someone will ask probing questions about what's going on in your life, appearing fascinated by every detail. Then, when he feels he's hit on a vulnerability, he throws acid on it. For example, you'll say you just got a great job at Acme Company. "Really?" the negative character will respond. "Aren't you worried about their falling profits? I heard that Nasty Company was going to try to buy them for peanuts and fire half the employees." You walk away feeling deflated.

In the end, negative people only end up hurting themselves. They lose opportunities they didn't even know were out there when the people they've scorched get their revenge by excluding them or becoming apathetic to their needs.

Finesse Requires Discipline

I once worked with an extremely intelligent woman who lamented her inability to relate to her colleagues or make polite conversation at industry events. When I questioned her, I learned that she made no effort to keep abreast of current trends—she didn't read magazines, go to movies, or watch television. Instead, she isolated herself in a world of opera and ballet. When I asked her why, she replied haughtily, "Pop culture is not interesting to me."

"It's interesting to *others,*" I told her. "If you want to talk to them, you have to demonstrate a regard for their favorite topics."

As I have stressed throughout this book, "Take me as I am" is the riskiest stance you can adopt when you're trying to bond with others and advance in business or social life. Whether that means staying glued to the TV or never turning it on, closing yourself off from others keeps them at a distance.

Don't Assume You Know Another Person's Rank

This is the mistake the arrogant account executive made on the plane returning from the Caribbean. Treat everyone as if he or she could be the best person you'll ever know and you can't make a mistake.

Earlier in my career I was the merchandise director of a textile firm. The chairman of one of our suppliers in Belgium arrived while our president was busy, so I received the visitor. I squired the chairman about and showed him our operation, turning on the charm. He was flattered by the attention and responded by inviting me to visit his factory as his guest in Belgium later that year.

I decided to accept his invitation during a trip to Europe several months later. Although it was off the beaten path, I traveled several hours out of my way to visit him. Upon arrival, I was greeted by two of his underlings, who hadn't bothered to give the chairman my message. They assumed I was of secondary importance and took me on a quickie tour of the factory.

My son, who spoke fluent French, was traveling with me. He listened as the men spoke to each other, then whispered to me that they were talking about how to get rid of me. Without telling them what David had heard, I insisted they take me to the chairman's office. He graciously apologized and explained that he had not been told I'd arrived.

Later in the year, these same gentlemen arrived in New York and called to meet with our executives. My assistant called me in confusion—the Belgian execs had been trying to arrange to have dinner with *him,* and he wanted to make sure I was included. When I told him the story of what had happened in Belgium, my assistant gleefully planned a gourmet dinner at a private club. Over dinner, the executives directed most of their attention to my assistant, until he finally informed them that I was in charge. They turned to me in shock, and it was then that I told them my son had understood their entire conversation back in Belgium. Need I say more?

Another story: One of the basic rules I set for my group sessions is that no one reveal any information about his or her background or level of power until the end of the day. That way the participants judge one another solely on the basis of personality. During one session, a woman bragged about putting herself through school and described how proud she was of how far she'd gotten on her own. She explained that she had no use for swells who were born with silver spoons in their mouths.

At the end of the seminar I pulled her aside and asked if there was anyone in the group she didn't particularly like. No, she said— in fact, she liked one woman so much she intended to ask her to lunch. "There's not much chance of that," I told her. "She's from an old distinguished family and your speech really turned her off. She didn't choose to be born into her family." In fact, she'd come to the seminar because she'd been so sheltered, and wanted to learn more about the mainstream of corporate life. The participant was flabbergasted—her reverse snobbery had offended a lovely, under-stated woman.

Real eagles don't have to flaunt their power. They understand noblesse oblige, the responsible behavior associated with high rank or birth, and conduct themselves with style, grace, and consider-ation for others.

SOAR WITH THE EAGLES

Adopt the principles outlined in this book and you'll become an eagle: flying free, flying high. The three-second impression others have of you will be a positive one, an impression that prompts them to share perks, offer information, and bring you into their circle of power. You will have the satisfaction that comes from knowing you've reached your potential and are contributing all you can to life.

There's a certain freedom that comes from scrutinizing yourself, seeing your assets and liabilities clearly, and remedying weak-nesses. Paradoxically, people who have taken this step stop being so hard on themselves. They learn empathy, both for themselves and for others. They accept the traits they cannot change while working to improve on their assets, all the while being patient with themselves. This generosity of spirit inspires them to bring pleasure into their own lives and into the lives of others while maintaining an increasingly positive attitude. Since people are drawn to pleasure and away from pain, I've watched as clients of mine attract more friends and business acquaintances than ever before.

Just as I ask my clients to take a long, hard look at themselves as a means of getting them to *stop* berating themselves, I ask them to focus on their hair and their shoes so that they can *stop* worrying about appearance. A famous newscaster once said that you have to know who you are before you know how to dress, and she's right. If you're settled in your identity and your place in the world, you stop fussing with your exterior.

An eagle does have concerns—paramount among these is his *reputation*. Once someone has defined himself and chosen a path, he focuses less on petty concerns and more on building esteem. Through altruistic acts, a person's good name becomes sacrosanct. Before seeking my help, a great many of my clients had never given their reputations much thought. After going through my program, they began to realize that the three-second impression defines what strangers think of them, and their reputations define what long-term observers say about them. If they've stayed out of the mud, their polished images and solid reputations will ensure that every door is open to them.

I emphasize that being a giver and being a wimp are two different things. An eagle is competitive—he just plays the game with decency. Taking advantage is not only permissible, it's necessary; determined people always grab the advantage. What separates them from the mosquitoes is that they follow the protocol that makes their tactics acceptable. Each of us must strike a balance between "looking out for number one" and giving. The return on your investment in your career is only worthwhile if you in turn do good with the advantages you've won.

Survival of the fittest is a principle that certainly applies to business, but in business the conquerors don't have to eat the dead for lunch. If they're eagles, they become mentors instead, sharing their knowledge and empowering others to achieve the same success. Or they share the wealth indirectly, through philanthropy.

Eagles have accepted the fact that the key to success is discipline; their reward is freedom. Freedom from financial worries, freedom to pursue life's pleasures, even freedom from regret. Eagles don't allow past mistakes or abuses to limit their potential. And the discipline they've developed has vaulted them into a realm where people often treat one another better. At the very least, they're less invasive and more considerate.

It's funny how progress isn't always a good thing. The sixties moved our society forward, but one side effect was the dawning of the Age of Informality. When it comes to clothing, it's nice to have the option to dress more comfortably. But when it comes to manners, it's not so nice to be treated discourteously.

Our society is moving past the time when older generations pass down their wisdom, including etiquette and manners. Pop culture now has a greater influence, and it espouses a civilization of narcissists, whose members get ahead by stepping on others. I don't endorse this nonsense.

I wrote *You've Only Got Three Seconds* to encourage you to share your talent with people at many levels. If you do it with empathy and style, you will fly with the eagles.

Index